MARCH

Make the Most of Every Month with Carson-Dellosa's Monthly Books!

Carson-Dellosa Publishing

Production Manager
Chris McIntyre

Editorial Director
Jennifer Weaver-Spencer

Writers
Lynette Pyne
Amy Gamble
Julie Eick Granchelli

Editors
Kelly Gunzenhauser
Carol Layton
Maria McKinney
Erin Proctor
Hank Rudisill

Art Directors
Pam Thayer
Alain Barsony
Penny Casto

Art Coordinator
J.J. Rudisill

Illustrators
Courtney Bunn
Amber Kocher Crouch
Mike Duggins
Erik Huffine
David Lackey
Ray Lambert
Wayne Miller
Bill Neville
Betsy Peninger
Dez Perrotti
Julie Webb

Cover Design
Amber Kocher Crouch
Ray Lambert
J.J. Rudisill

Carson-Dellosa Publishing Company, Inc.

MARCH

Table of Contents

MARCH TEACHER TIPS

Direct Attention

Avoid wandering minds when a student is speaking. Stand at the opposite end of the room from the talking student. Placing the rest of the class between the teacher and the speaker will encourage the rest of the students to pay attention and be involved in the discussion.

Signal for Help

Students will work more independently when using help signals. Give each child two plastic cups—one red and one green. While completing desk work, have each student stack his cups on his desktop. When the student understands the assignment and is working smoothly, have him place the green cup on top. If a student needs help, have him place the red cup on top. Check the room periodically for students who need assistance.

Return that Homework!

Are students forgetting to turn in spelling homework? Use the bonus jar to focus on responsibility! On a slip of paper, write the name of each student who turns in all spelling homework. Place the names in a jar. On the day of the spelling test, draw a name from the jar and give that student an automatic "A." Students will have incentive to be more careful about turning in homework!

Rewarding Responsibility

To show confidence in students, give each student 20 responsibility points at the beginning of each week. When a student forgets homework, does not have a pencil, etc., delete a predetermined number of points. At the end of the week, reward students with more than 15 points remaining.

Smooth Sailing for Substitutes

Make your substitutes' days run smoothly by assigning student helpers. The day before an absence, call one student at home and ask him to be the special substitute helper. Choose a student who is not usually a class leader to help build confidence and self-esteem.

Pictures Say a Thousand Words

Involve parents in their children's school day. Use a digital camera to photograph students participating in class activities, then e-mail them to parents. Photographs may also be placed in a take-home folder. Have one student at a time take home the folder. When all parents have seen the photos, replace them with new ones and route the folder again.

March Day-by-Day Calendar

1 *National Craft Month* To celebrate, make small crafts, such as button picture frames, with the class. Put the crafts on display for the entire month.

2 *Read Across America Day* Have students read short books and give book reports.

3 *Alexander Graham Bell's Birthday* He was born on this day in 1847. Have students list five reasons they might use the telephone.

4 *National Write a Letter of Appreciation Week* is March 1-7. Brainstorm a list of school employees who deserve an appreciation letter. Let students pick one and write to that person.

5 *International Day of the Seal* Celebrate by teaching seal facts: their closest relatives are land mammals like dogs and cats, seals spend most of their lives in water, etc.

6 *Michelangelo's Birthday* The famous painter and sculptor was born today in 1475. Give students clay and have them mold a sculpture of their own.

7 *Autograph Collecting Week* is March 7-13. Make autograph books with the class. Then, have a signing party.

8 *International Working Women's Day* This holiday was designed to honor working women. Have each student select a woman he knows and write about her job or career.

9 *Artificial teeth* were *patented* on this day in 1822. Discuss dental health with students and have them write why it is important to take care of their teeth.

10 *Paper money was first issued in the U.S.* on this date in 1862. Have students make paper money. Use the money as manipulatives in math activities.

THE UNITED STATES OF AMERICA
1 · Washington · ONE DOLLAR · 1

11 *Ezra Jack Keats' Birthday* Make some of his books, such as *A Letter to Amy*; *Hi, Cat!*; and *Dreams*, available to students in a reading center.

12 *Optimism Month* Make a *We're Positive* bulletin board. Give students construction paper stars with the phrase *I'm positive that....* Ask each student to fill in the blank with a positive statement or short-term goal.

13 The planet *Uranus was discovered* on this day in 1781 by astronomer William Herschel. Have students research the origins of the names of the planets.

14 *Albert Einstein's Birthday* The scientist was born today in 1879. Have students think about careers in science. Generate a class list and have each student suggest what area of science he likes and why.

15 *National Umbrella Month* Have students draw humorous pictures of umbrella substitutes that people might use if the umbrella had never been invented.

16 **Red Cross Month** Have students research the Red Cross. Then, have them create a banner honoring this organization. Donate the banner to a local Red Cross office.

17 **Rubber bands were invented** today in 1845. Brainstorm a class list of as many uses for the rubber band as possible.

18 **Absolutely Incredible Kid Day** Put each student's name in a hat. Have each child draw a name and write or tell three good things about that student.

19 **Swallows Day** Thousands of swallows make their annual return to the Mission at San Juan Capistrano. Look up *migration* in the dictionary and read the definition aloud. Brainstorm a list of other migrating animals.

20 **Smile Rejuvenation Day** Have students write shape smile poems telling what makes them smile.

friends bring a smile to my face.

21 **Johann Sebastian Bach's Birthday** He was born today in 1685. Listen to a piece of music by this famous composer.

22 **International Goof-Off Day** Set aside some time today for the class to just "goof off."

23 **Roger Bannister's Birthday** The first runner to run a mile in less than four minutes was born on this day in 1929. Challenge students to run in place for four minutes.

24 **Harry Houdini's Birthday** The magician was born today in 1874. Teach the class a simple magic trick, such as "Pick a Card," in his honor.

25 **Pecan Day** Commemorate the day George Washington planted pecan trees at Mount Vernon by bringing in pecans to enjoy with the class.

26 **Robert Frost's Birthday** The poet was born in 1874. Share the picture book *Stopping by Woods on a Snowy Evening*. Then, have students write poems about spring.

27 **Youth Art Month** Show students several art books. Have students draw pictures emulating their favorite art style.

28 **Byrd Baylor's Birthday** The children's author was born today in 1924. Read her book *Everybody Needs a Rock*. Take students outside to look for rocks. Let students paint the rocks to create "pet rocks."

29 **National Sleep Awareness Week** begins the last week in March. Brainstorm a list of important reasons to get a good night's sleep. Have students decorate copies of the list to take home.

30 **Vincent Van Gogh's Birthday** The painter was born today in 1853. Show students a picture of his famous painting, *Sunflowers*, and have them paint pictures of their favorite flowers in a similar fashion.

31 **The first dance marathon in the United States** was **held today** in New York City in 1923. Teach the class a dance or allow them to dance freestyle in honor of this occasion.

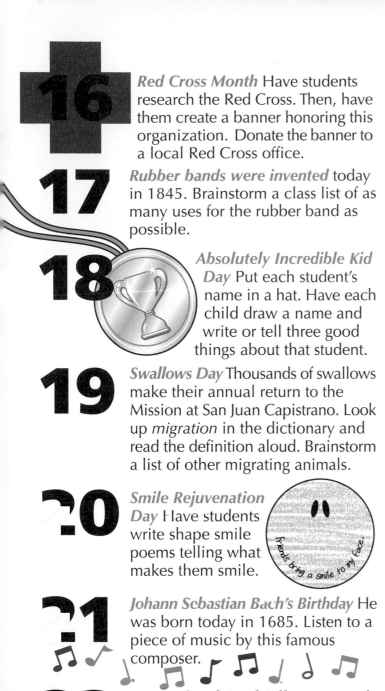

5

March

Sunday	Monday	Tuesday	Wednesday	Thursday	Friday	Saturday

March Gazette

Teacher _____ Date _____

IN THE NEWS

TAKE NOTE

WHAT'S COMING UP

KID'S CORNER
Color the kite.

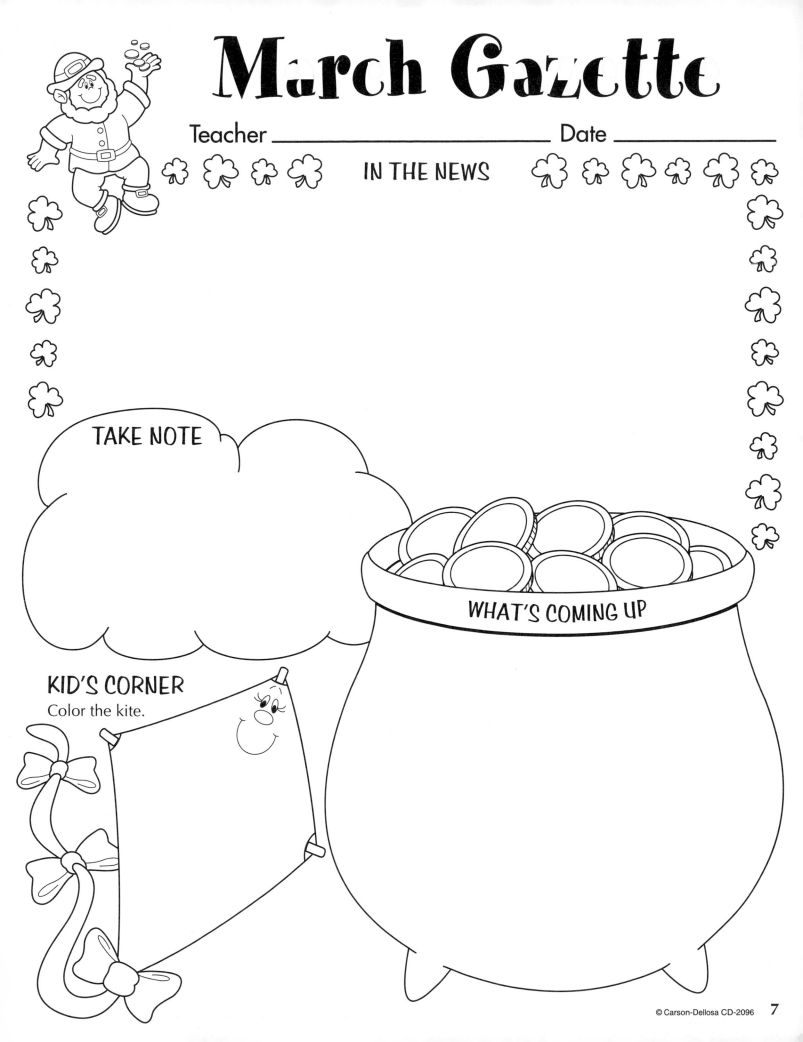

7

Celebrate March!

Dear Family Members,
Here are a few quick-and-easy activities to help you and your child celebrate special days throughout the month of March.

March is *National Craft Month*
- Share a favorite craft with your child, such as sewing, woodworking, or quilting. Plan a project and let your child work with you to finish it.

Youth Art Month is celebrated in March
- Help your child make a special frame for a select piece of artwork. Display the framed artwork on a wall at home.

March 1-7 is *National Write a Letter of Appreciation Week*
- Encourage your child to think of someone he or she appreciates, such as a teacher, family member, or coach. Have your child write a letter expressing thanks to that person for the help and encouragement.

Absolutely Incredible Kid Day is the third Thursday in March.
- Set aside some time today to tell your child why he or she is an absolutely incredible kid!

March 22 is *International Goof-Off Day*
- Celebrate by taking time away from household chores to do something fun as a family.

Pecan Day is March 25
- Follow the recipe below to enjoy some tasty candied pecans with your child.
  - 1 teaspoon cold water
  - 1 egg white
  - 1 pound large pecan halves
  - 1 cup sugar
  - 1 teaspoon cinnamon
  - 1 teaspoon salt

Beat water and egg white together until frothy. Mix in pecans. Combine sugar, cinnamon, and salt. Stir into pecan mixture. Spread on a cookie sheet. Bake at 225° for 1 hour, stirring occasionally.

National Sleep Awareness Week begins the last week of March
- Get the benefits of a good night's sleep by having everyone in the family go to bed earlier. Before retiring, spend some quiet time together reading or listening to soft music.

Read In March!

Dear Family Members,
Here are some books to share with your child to enhance the enjoyment of reading in March.

 My Spring Robin by Anne Rockwell
- *A girl discovers many signs of spring as she searches for her spring robin.*
- Read the story, then go for a walk with your child. Take a notepad and pencil and record all the signs of spring you see on your outing, including (hopefully) a robin!

 Mud by Mary Lyn Ray
- *Vivid illustrations and text reveal the joys of playing in the warm spring mud.*
- Prepare "mud" (chocolate pudding) for your child to eat while you share this book together.

 Jamie O'Rourke and the Big Potato by Tomie dePaola
- *A leprechaun grants Jamie his wish for a big potato. When the potato blocks the road, the townspeople have to eat potato all winter and beg Jamie not to plant another.*
- After reading the story, ask your child to imagine what would grow from a seed that was a gift from a leprechaun. Have you child tell what happens in his version of this tale.

 Leprechaun Gold by Teresa Bateman
- *After saving a leprechaun, Donald O'Dell refuses his gold but is rewarded with something even better.*
- Read the story and make a list with your child of things that are better than gold.

 Lucky O'Leprechaun by Jana Dillon
- *With the help of their aunties, Sara and Meg outwit a leprechaun. They do not wish for his gold, but instead wish that he would spend St. Patrick's Day with them every year.*
- The children want the leprechaun to return each year to answer their questions. Have your child make a list of questions he or she would like to ask a leprechaun. While your child is asleep, list the answers with a green pencil and leave a St. Patrick's day treat with the list.

 The Gift of Driscoll Lipscomb by Sara Yamaka
- *Each year on her birthday, the narrator receives a gift from her artist neighbor—a brush with one color of paint. After several birthdays, she has all the colors in the rainbow.*
- Paint a rainbow picture with your child. As he or she adds each color, have your child list as many things as possible that are that color. Hang the picture in your child's bedroom to brighten each day.

A Rainbow of My Own by Don Freeman
- *A small boy imagines what it would be like to have his own rainbow to play with.*
- Create a rainbow with your child. After reading the story, fill a glass with water and place it in a sunny window. Move the glass until a rainbow appears on the walls or floor.

9

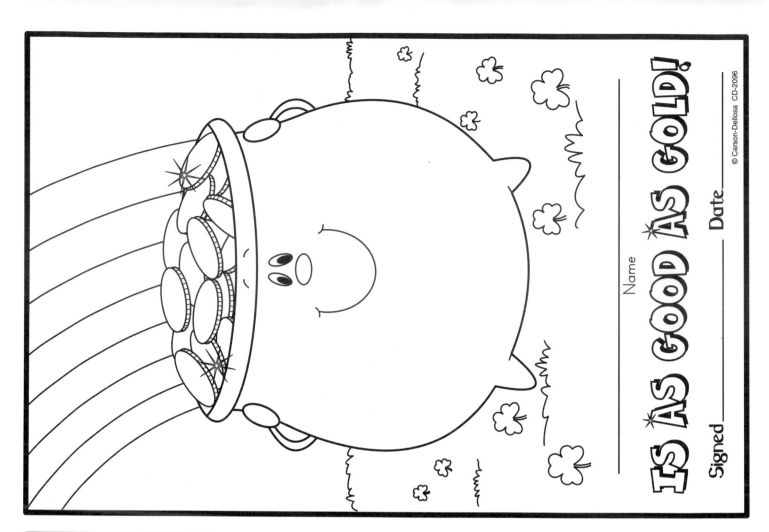

IS AS GOOD AS GOLD!

Name _____

Signed _____ Date _____

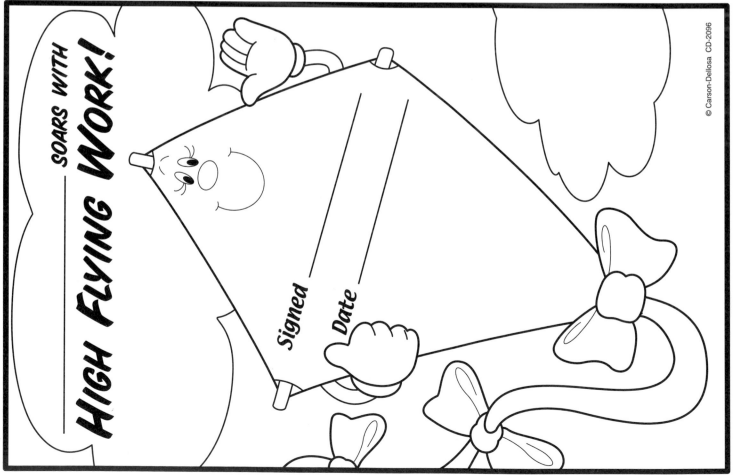

SOARS WITH HIGH FLYING WORK!

Signed _____

Date _____

WOW!

HAD A GOOD DAY!

Name _____

Signed _____   Date _____

_____ is a
SUPER CITIZEN!

Signed _____   Date _____

MARCH
Writing Activities

In March, winter begins to loosen its icy grip. Keep students' skills sharp as everyone anxiously watches for the first signs of spring. Set enough time aside in students' writing schedules to include both group work and individual activities.

Word Bank Words

wind	nest
shamrock	birdhouse
leprechaun	crocus
spring	daffodil
lion	rainbow
Ireland	lucky
lamb	kite
robin	green

Stormy Weather

Animals are used to describe March weather, but March weather can also describe animals. Have students each pick a favorite pet or other animal to describe. Then, think of weather conditions that could be used to describe the animal. For example: *My cat is lazy like a rainy day. Sometimes she races around the house like lightning. She scares me like thunder when she jumps on my bed in the middle of the night.*

Leprechaun's Gold

Having trouble catching up with a leprechaun? Write him a letter. Have students write letters to a leprechaun persuading him to share his gold. Students can explain why they should get the gold and what they would do with it. Have them seal their letters in envelopes decorated with gold and rainbows, then place the letters under a bush near the school. At the end of the day, gather the letters and write short responses to each on shamrock patterns (page 77), saying why you (the leprechaun) think they are all too deserving to choose just one—so you'll have to keep the gold! If desired, substitute a gift of a gold foil-covered chocolate for the real thing.

Story Jar

Give students the opportunity to learn more about their classmates with a story jar. Write personal topics, such as *My favorite place is...,* or *After school, I...,* on slips of paper and place in a jar. At writing time, let each student pick a slip from the jar and write a personal narrative on the chosen topic. Let students share their stories, then return the slips to the jar. Have students periodically pick new topics from the jar.

Picture Perfect

Turn things around in your writing classroom! Instead of having students illustrate after writing a story, let them illustrate before they write. Without telling students they will be writing a story, have them each draw and color a picture of their choice on white paper. If desired, let students exchange drawings. Then, tell students to look at the pictures and think about what is happening in the scenes. Based on the illustrations, challenge students to write imaginative stories to accompany the pictures. Display the pictures, then have each student read his story and let the class guess which picture matches it.

Make a List

Are your students listless journal writers? Add some lists to their journals! List-making can boost memory and provide spelling and observation practice. Provide a different topic each day, such as *things in a classroom* or *toys I have*. Challenge students to develop of list of as many words as possible that fit the category.

Poster Poems

Welcome spring to your classroom by displaying a colorful spring-themed poster (flowers, rainbow, etc.) Ask each student to look at the poster and write a poem using it as inspiration. They may wish to describe the scene in their poems, or write about how they feel as they look at it. Provide spring-colored paper for students to copy their finished poems on, then arrange the poems around the poster, creating a cheerful spring display.

Senior Editors

Free up your time during writing activities by assigning students to be senior editors. Choose two or three students each weeks to be the official editors and help their classmates with their writing. Students can come go to the senior editors and ask for help with spelling, grammar, and story ideas Encourage senior editors to use the dictionary and to ask each student questions about his characters and plot to help him get past any writing difficulties.

I enjoyed reading your paper!
-Senior Editor

SPELLING REVIEW

Turn studying spelling words into fun and games! Divide the class into 4-5 groups and number students so each group has a number 1 student, a number 2 student, etc. Call a number and have each student with that number go to the chalkboard. Call out a spelling word. The first student to spell the word correctly on the board wins a point for her team. Give each member of the winning team a bonus point on the weekly spelling test.

Bulletin Board Ideas

Spring knowledge is for the birds! Provide enlarged bird patterns (page 28) and egg and nest shapes for students. Decorate a bulletin board with a paper tree and tissue paper leaves and flowers. Let small groups research different types of area birds and their eggs. Have students color nest shapes and label them with the bird types, then color the birds and eggs and place them in the nests. If desired, have older students research diet, migration, etc., and add these facts to the nests as well. Use with the *Spring Fever* chapter (pages 20-28).

Shower students with praise for their good poetry! Enlarge the umbrella top and umbrella handle patterns (page 27) on construction paper and post on a bulletin board. Let students color raindrop patterns (page 27). Then, let students write spring haikus. Accent the poems with raindrops, and post them during your study of the *Spring Fever* chapter (pages 20-28).

EXCEPTIONAL WOMEN!

She was the first American woman to win three gold medals in a single Olympics.

She was a famous American Impressionist artist.

She invented the first chocolate chip cookie.

She refused to sit at the back of a bus and fueled the Civil Rights Movement.

She was the first female U.S. Supreme Court Justice.

She discovered radium and won two Nobel Prizes.

She was an interpreter, guide and peacemaker for the Lewis and Clarke expedition.

She was the first woman in space.

Labels: Marie Curie · Sandra Day O'Connor · Famous Portraits · Wilma Rudolph · Mary Cassatt · Ruth Wakefield · Rosa Parks · Sacajawea · Valentina Tereshkova

What did these women do? To find out, post student-drawn symbols (and photos, if desired) representing the accomplishments of famous women listed in the *Women's History Month* chapter (pages 29-36). For example, post an artist's palette for Mary Cassatt, a spaceship for Valentina Tereshkova, etc. On each illustration, write clues to the woman's identity, but do not list her name. Write the names on sentence strips, attach a piece of string to each, then thumbtack to the board. Let students match the women's portraits and names to their symbols and achievements.

1000 B.C.-Chinese Kites

1783-Hot Air Balloon

1903-Airplane

1907-Helicopter

FLYING TO THE FUTURE

2050- Future Flying Machines

Fly away to the future with fantastic flying machines! In construction paper clouds, post pictures of flying machines in chronological order. Then, let students invent and illustrate new flying machines. Post their inventions to complement the activities in the *Catch the Wind* chapter (pages 37-47).

15

CLASS 304 NEWS

Vol. 1

March 12, 2008

Mrs. Franklin's Class Storms the Zoo!

by Olivia Thayer

On March 21st, Mrs. Franklin, our super-duper teacher, took our class to the city zoo. It was exciting for everyone, except Mindy Craig who got sick in the morning and had to call her mom to pick her up. Sorry Mindy! We saw many animals, including monkeys, birds, polar bears, snakes, lions, elephants, and giraffes. The scariest part was when all the chimpanzees got into a fight and started screeching. They made us back away from the cages then. But I'll let Justin tell about that.

picture by Rebecca Wheeler

New Aviary a Success

by Trang Nguyen

During our trip to the zoo, we went through a brand new building. The building was a large, glass dome. Inside, it was very quiet and warm. There were huge jungle plants everywhere. The aviary is the newest exhibit at the zoo, and it is a lot of fun. Swoop! Something flew past my face! It was a huge, blue parrot. Standing near us were pretty pink flamingos. The whole room was full of bright birds. Some of them had nests high in the trees. The class became very quiet while walking through the aviary. I asked if the birds ever escaped. The zookeeper said, "Not yet, but we have to be very careful with them at feeding time. They might try to follow the zookeeper with extra food back into the main building and then we would be trying to capture them!"

Justin Sees the Monkeys

by Justin Roberts

I was having a good time at the zoo with the class. The monkey feeder walked up to the monkey's area with a banana in her hand to give to one of the monkeys. She gave it to one monkey that wanted it first. All the other monkeys wanted it too. They tried to grab it from the monkey she gave it too, and started screeching! Then the monkey feeder made me and the class back away from the cages. She gave them some more bananas, and they stopped screeching. She went into the monkey's area to give them the rest of their food. It was exciting!

New Babies at the Zoo

by LaShonda Martin

There were a lot of new babies at the zoo last week! The boa constrictor mother had 32 new babies. They were all over the place. The zookeeper in the reptile area said that the mother snake was three years old, and that the babies had just eaten for the first time. Soon, they will go to other zoos. Some will stay at our zoo, and the zookeeper said we could write letters or send e-mail to enter a contest to name the babies. I want to name one Jeffery.

picture by Te-Anne Cahill

Document the next class field trip with a special edition bulletin board newspaper. Roll sheets of newspaper to use as a border. Then, assign different students to write articles about the field trip. Let other students illustrate the articles. Post the articles and illustrations on the board in a newspaper format, complete with headline, volume number, date, captions, etc. If desired, invite other classes to see the field trip headlines. During the *Newspapers in Education* unit (pages 48-52), leave the board as is, or change it with updated news, leaving the heading of the board intact.

We will read books every day. We will read books if we may! Use the familiar book *The Cat in the Hat* to measure how many Dr. Seuss books are read during the *Read with Dr. Seuss* chapter (pages 53-59). Trace an enlarged hat pattern (page 59) on black paper and post on a bulletin board. On red and white sentence strips, write the names of each Dr. Seuss books the class will read. As each book is read, post the strip on the hat, alternating colors. When the hat is full, celebrate by allowing the class to vote on which book they would like to read again.

Helping out creates harmony! Cut several strips of different colored butcher paper the length of the bulletin board, and attach them so that they overlap horizontally. Draw a marker treble clef and time signature (see page 68 for reference). Have children draw pictures of themselves performing helpful tasks, such as passing out papers or putting away books. Accent the drawings with enlarged note patterns (page 68). Use this board to coincide with the *Making Music in Our Schools* chapter (pages 62-68).

Kids will never forget how lucky they are while learning about St. Patrick's Day (pages 69-78)! Enlarge several four-leaf clover patterns (page 77). Give one to each child and have him write and illustrate a reason why he is lucky. Post the clovers on a grass background, and accent with a leprechaun pattern (page 77)!

17

MR. ALLEN'S CLASS IS PURE GOLD!

Pam
Pam
9+1 = 10
2+5 = 7
9+2 = 11
1+4 = 5
6+2 = 8
8+6 = 14

Hugh
High.
March Words
1. shamrock
2. clover
3. lion
4. lamb
5. wind
6. green
7. gold

Beth

MARCH

Melissa
MELISSA
5+1 = 6
7+5 = 12
9+6 = 15
4+4 = 8
6+7 = 13
2+6 = 8

Lynn
Lynn
In March we get to celebrate St. Patrick's Day. You have to wear green to school that day. If you forget everyone is allowed to give you a small pinch.

Christina
Christina
I love the month of March! My birthday is March 13th. This year I am going to be seven years old. St. Patrick's Day is four days after my birthday.

Scott
SCOTT
5+1 = 6
7+5 = 12
9+6 = 15
4+4 = 8
6+7 = 13
2+6 = 8

Todd
Todd
March Words
1. leprechaun
2. lucky
3. green
4. pot-o-gold
5. rainbow
6. shamrock
7. windy

Tyler

Celebrate students' golden work during *St. Patrick's Day* (pages 69-78) celebrations! Cut the top of a pot of gold pattern (page 78) from black construction paper. Make a streamer rainbow, then fill the pot and make a border from gold coin patterns copied onto shiny paper (page 76). Add construction paper backers in rainbow colors to student work, then post and accent with more gold coins.

Show how two heads are better than one. Pair students and give each pair two paintbrush patterns (page 84). Have them interview each other about hobbies, skills, and talents that they share, such as playing together on a sports team or belonging to the same after-school club. Have each student in the pair color her brush a different primary color, and label with her name. Finally, let the pair choose a color of construction paper that matches the mixed primary colors on their brushes, then cut out a puddle shape. Have students write the task they can complete together on the puddle. Post the paintbrushes and puddles on the bulletin board during your study of *Rainbows and Colors* (pages 79-84).

WE MIX WELL!

Jennifer and Alex like to draw.

Mark and Leon are vegetarians.

Chang and Alyssa both have pet parakeets.

LaShawnda pitches and Carmen catches for the softball team.

Mary and David love to read mysteries.

Owen and Madison like to play the piano.

Capture colorful objects with this bright display. Cut two ovals from blue and brown butcher paper, making the blue oval slightly smaller than the brown oval. Overlap them to make a magnifying glass lens. Then, create a paper handle. Label the lens *I See Something*. Attach butcher paper strips in the colors and order of the spectrum, so that a rainbow appears to be shining out of the lens. Label each strip with its color name. During the *Rainbows and Colors* chapter (pages 79-84), have students cut out photographs of colorful objects, and post them in the corresponding strips. You may wish to allow students to write words on the strips as well.

Encourage your students to eat a balanced diet during the *Food for Thought* chapter (pages 85-92). Cut out rectangle and circle shapes to assemble a bulletin-board sized paper scale as shown. Post each food group, along with its recommended number of daily servings, on one side of the scale. Let students bring in or cut out pictures of foods. Using the serving information, let small groups take turns attaching pictures above the scale to make the correct number of servings for each food group. When a group has posted all of the foods, have students help you check for the correct number of servings in each food group.

SPRING FEVER

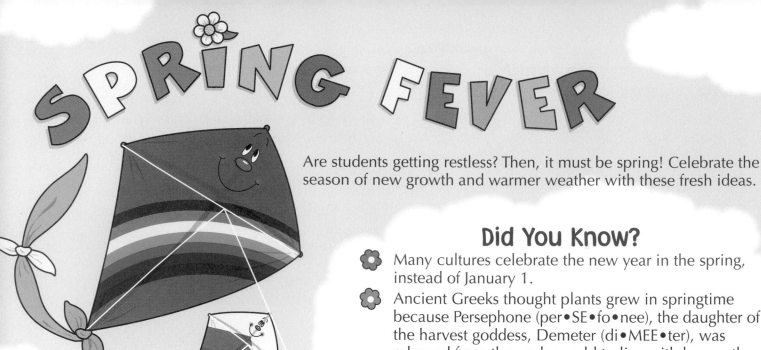

Are students getting restless? Then, it must be spring! Celebrate the season of new growth and warmer weather with these fresh ideas.

Did You Know?

❀ Many cultures celebrate the new year in the spring, instead of January 1.

❀ Ancient Greeks thought plants grew in springtime because Persephone (per•SE•fo•nee), the daughter of the harvest goddess, Demeter (di•MEE•ter), was released from the underworld to live with her mother until autumn, when she returned to Hades (HAY•dees) and plant life died.

Literature Selections

Hopper Hunts for Spring by Marcus Pfister: North-South Books, 1992. (Picture book, 32 pg.) Soft watercolors depict a bunny's search for a friend, Spring, whom his mother has told him is coming.
Mud by Mary Lyn Ray: Harcourt Brace & Co., 1996. (Picture book, 32 pg.) Vivid illustrations and text reveal the joys of warm spring mud.
My Spring Robin by Anne Rockwell: Aladdin Publishing Company, 1996. (Picture book, 24 pg.) A girl searches for a spring robin.
Spring by Ron Hirschi: Penguin Putnam Books for Young Readers, 1990. (Picture book, 32 pg.) Photographs depict wild animals in springtime.
Spring Thaw by Steven Schnur: Viking Penguin, 2000. (Picture book, 32 pg.) Signs of spring appear as snow and ice melt away.
Sugarbush Spring by Marsha Wilson Chall: Lothrop, Lee & Shepard, 2000. (Picture book, 24 pg.) A family in Minnesota collects spring sap to make maple syrup.

Spring Journal

Capture spring in these special journals. Cut large leaf shapes from spring green paper. Punch two holes along the bottom of the leaves and thread a rubber band through, back to front. Slide a twig through the loops of rubber band sticking out from each hole in the front. Tuck spring flowers made from tissue paper under the rubber band loops to hide them. Finally, take students for a spring walk and have them draw or write about signs of spring in their journals.

Dear Spring,
I can't wait until you're here! The flowers in our yard are always so pretty when you're around. I'm lookin...

March 21, 2003

Sincerely,
LILY

Say Good-Bye to Winter

Saying hello to spring means saying good-bye to winter. Brainstorm a list of things associated with winter that students enjoy, such as sledding, snow days, holidays, etc., and a list of things they enjoy about spring, such as warm weather, flowers blooming, etc. Have students write letters to winter saying farewell and describing all the winter things they will miss during spring. Have them decorate their letters with wintry pictures. Then, turn the papers over and write letters to spring, describing all the things they are anticipating about its arrival. Decorate this side with spring pictures. Finally, let each child read her letters to the class. Display the letters together on a bulletin board titled, *Good-bye winter! Hello spring!*

Spring Equinox

Anticipate the first day of spring by tracking the number of daylight and nighttime hours until they are equal. Explain that the first day of spring, which falls in the third week of March, is called the vernal equinox (there is also an autumnal equinox in September). *Equinox* means "equal night," because the number of hours in the day and the number of hours in the night are equal. Provide a newspaper each day during the week before the vernal equinox and have students record daily sunrise and sunset information. Based on this information, have them calculate how long the days and nights were. Point out that the daylight increased, and tell students that daylight will continue to increase until the summer solstice in June, then decrease until the winter solstice in December.

Animal Weather Posters

March's weather may come in like a lion and go out like a lamb, but what about December or June? Brainstorm lists of animals and weather conditions with students. Talk about which weather conditions are most like which animals. Challenge each student to make up her own animal saying associated with the weather in a particular month. Each student can create a poster with the name of the month at the top, her saying at the bottom, and a picture depicting the saying in the center. Display the posters in calendar order around the room.

January is like a polar bear.

It is ready to roar!

Lion and Lamb Magnets

See at a glance whether students think a March day is a lion or lamb day when they display these desk magnets. Have each child make a lion magnet and a lamb magnet, then complete the weather tracking activity, *In Like a Lion, Out Like a Lamb* (below).

To make a lion magnet:

1. Cut a 2¼" circle from poster board and one from light brown or orange felt. Glue the felt over the poster board. Glue a 1" yellow button in the center of the felt circle.
2. Knot yellow and brown yarn together. Leave ½" on either side of the knot. Make 12 knots and glue to the edge of the poster board circle.
3. Glue a yellow pony bead to the middle of the button and use white paint and a black marker to draw a lion face on the button.
4. Secure magnetic tape to the back.

To make a lamb magnet:

1. Cut a 2" oval from white poster board. Cut a black pipe cleaner in half and bend into two legs. Glue to the poster board oval.
2. Glue a cotton ball to the oval, covering the poster board and partially covering the legs.
3. Glue a black button to the center of the cotton ball and glue a black pony bead to the center of the button.
4. Cut ears from black felt and glue to each side of the button. Use white paint and a black marker to draw a face on the button.
5. Secure magnetic tape to the back.

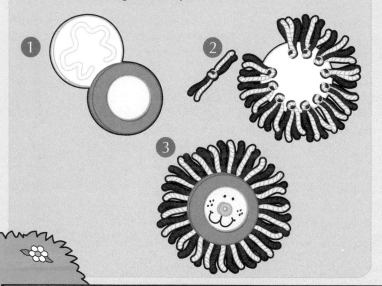

In Like a Lion, Out Like a Lamb

Conduct an experiment to test the old adage about March coming in like a lion and going out like a lamb. Discuss the types of weather students think would be associated with each animal. Then, enlarge the March calendar grid (page 6) and mount on poster board. Each day, ask students to observe the weather, then display the lamb or lion magnets (see *Lion and Lamb Magnets,* above) on the fronts of their desks. Have a student tally the votes each day and make a thumbprint lion or lamb on the calendar, depending on the winning magnet. At the end of the month, look for patterns, compare the number of lion days vs. lamb days, and see if March came in like a lion and went out like a lamb. When March is over, send the magnets home for children to enjoy.

22

Spring is in the air.
Birds migrate north.

Spring is on the ground.
Tree branches burst with
fluffy blooms.

Spring is underground.
Earthworms move, past
the curling seeds.

MIKE

Spring Poems Are in the Air

Look for signs of spring to inspire students to write poetry. Have students follow the model at left to write poems about the springtime things they observe in the air, on the ground, and in the ground. Let each child divide a piece of paper into three horizontal sections and draw a spring scene, divided into air, ground (grass, shrubs, and trees), and underground sections. Let students write two lines of their poems in each section.

Crocus Card

These earliest flowers of spring will add springtime cheer to greeting cards. Have each student turn a sheet of white paper horizontally and cut off the top third in a wavy line. Tape the edges of the remaining sheet of white paper to a light blue piece of paper, creating a pocket (do not tape the wavy edge). Fold in half, draw a spring picture on the front of the card, and write a message on the white paper "snow" inside. Next, make two crocuses which will pop out of the snow. Students can trace and cut out eight crocus petal patterns (page 28) from yellow or purple paper. Use the same color marker to draw ribs along each petal. Cut out two crocus pistil patterns (page 28) from yellow or orange paper and glue them to the top of the petals. Glue the petals together, overlapping as shown at right. Make a stem and long leaves from green paper and glue to the bloom. Tuck the crocuses into the pocket so that the recipient of the card can pull them out of the snow. Spring has sprung!

Spring is popping up!

Have a happy spring day!
Love,
Sara

Fact Flowers

Create fact flowers and make narcissus bulbs bloom in your classroom! Assign small groups of students and give each group a narcissus bulb. Have each group poke three toothpicks into a bulb and balance it on top of a plastic cup. Fill the cup with water. The bottom of the bulb should be in the water at all times. Label the cups with group names and place them in a windowsill. Bulbs should take about a week to sprout.

As students take measurements and record observations about their bulbs, let them display their findings on construction paper flower petals to create fact flowers. Give each group a yellow circle. Have the group write its name on the circle, then staple to a bulletin board atop a green paper stem with leaves. Provide large, white, petal-shaped papers. Have the group record the information on petals and attach them around the yellow circle. At the end of the month, not only will the real flowers be blooming, but so will the fact flowers!

March 8
There are some tiny roots on the bottom!

March 7
We watered the flower. Nothing yet.

March 6
Today we set up our flowers.

GROUP A
Rebecca   Julie
John   Te-Anne

23

Cherry Blossom Festival

Each spring, visitors flock to Washington, D.C. to celebrate the National Cherry Blossom Festival, commemorating the gift from Tokyo of 3,000 cherry trees. The celebration includes a parade, tree plantings, and a Japanese cultural festival. Hold a class Cherry Blossom Festival and let students learn more about Japanese life. Prepare for the festival by cutting strips of brown paper and circles of green paper and arranging them on boards and walls to look like trees. Next, shake popped popcorn in a plastic bag with pink tempera paint. Let students help put the room in full bloom by gluing the popcorn to the "trees" to resemble pink cherry blossoms. Then, set a date for the classroom festival. Assign groups of students to study and report on aspects of Japanese life, such as food, dress, arts, etc. On festival day, invite parents and other classes to view the cherry blossoms and learn about Japan.

Pussy Willows

Pussy willows announce the coming of spring with the growth of soft *catkins* on their branches. Let students create soft pussy willow pictures to celebrate. Have students make the ground a combination of snow and spring grass by tearing pieces of green and white paper and gluing them to the bottom of a light blue piece of paper, then draw brown branches coming up from the ground. Cut off ends of cotton swabs. Students can complete the pictures by gluing the soft tips to the branches to represent the catkins. When the glue is dry, students can feel their soft pussy willow trees as you tell them the legend of the pussy willow (below).

The Legend of the Pussy Willow:

Long ago a willow tree heard a mother cat crying because her kittens had fallen in the river. The willow tree felt so badly that it bent its branches into the river to catch the kittens. The kittens held on tightly and were pulled to shore. Now, each year the willow sprouts soft, furry buds where the kittens held on.

What's in the Grass?

As spring warms the ground, bugs and creepy crawlies come out to play. Set up a center in the classroom for students to discover what is in the grass. Place a low, wide box on a table and fill it with green Easter grass. In the grass, hide a variety of plastic bugs, worms, snakes, turtles, etc. Then, place several magnifying glasses near the box and let students examine the grass. Have students record their observations in a science journal. If desired, have each student choose one creature he observed to research. Let students write reports, share their observations, and tell why they think these animals are active in the spring grass.

24

Robin Redbreast

Robins are one of the first birds to migrate north in the spring and are considered a sign that spring has arrived. Signal the start of spring by letting students make these paper plate round robins.

1. For the robin's body, divide a paper plate with a curved line. Color the large portion red and the small portion brown.
2. Divide another paper plate to form the wing, tail, and nest. Color brown and cut out.
3. Glue the tail on the side of the bird's body. Attach the wing to the body with a paper fastener. Cut an oval shape from poster board for a head, and color brown. Glue the head to the top of the plate.
4. Draw eyes and glue on a yellow paper diamond, folded in half to make a beak. Make a brown paper worm and glue to the beak.
5. To make the nest, cut a few blue paper eggs and glue them to the inside curve of the nest. Fill in around the eggs with sticks, string, etc.
6. Glue the robin in the nest, matching up the ridges in the rim of the body plate to the ridges in the nest section.

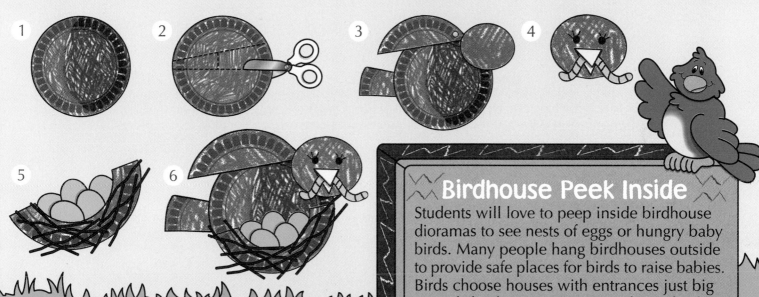

Bird Nest Materials

Provide cozy materials to help birds build their nests. In the spring, birds migrate home after their winter vacations and start building nests for their eggs, using whatever materials they can find. Have students bring in mesh produce bags, string and yarn (shorter than 6" so they do not entangle the birds), dryer lint, and fabric. Pair students and let each pair stuff a mesh bag with hay, grass, and small twigs, along with the manmade materials. Hang the bags with twist-ties from branches of trees and shrubs, keeping in mind that some birds build their nests high and some build their nests low. Let several days pass, then check the bags to see if any materials have been used. Also, check the area for bird nests that may include some of students' nest materials.

Birdhouse Peek Inside

Students will love to peep inside birdhouse dioramas to see nests of eggs or hungry baby birds. Many people hang birdhouses outside to provide safe places for birds to raise babies. Birds choose houses with entrances just big enough for them to enter so no larger birds or animals can threaten the nest inside. Give each child a shoebox with a small hole cut in the lid, to decorate like a birdhouse. Next, cut a slit below the hole and insert a craft stick as the perch. Give each child a bird pattern (page 28) to cut out, decorate, and glue to the perch. Let children open their boxes and create bird nests from sticks, string, etc. Complete the nests with paper eggs and baby birds. Older students can research and replicate specific birds' nests, egg colors, etc. Staple the boxes to a bulletin board and replace the fronts. Staple brown paper posts below each birdhouse. Let students take turns removing the lids and peeking inside.

25

Under the Umbrella

Check out who is keeping dry under these spring umbrellas! Give each child a sheet of light colored paper. Have him fold it in half and trace the umbrella top pattern (page 27), placing the top of the umbrella on the fold. Cut out the umbrella top, leaving an inch of the fold intact. Let students decorate the fronts and backs of their umbrellas and cut out and tape umbrella handle patterns (page 27) inside. Then, have each child glue a photo or draw a picture of himself inside the umbrella. Punch a hole in the center of the fold, thread a long string through the hole, and knot it on the inside of the umbrella. Next, cut several raindrop patterns (page 27) from blue paper. Tape a different length of string to each raindrop. Tie the ends of all the string (including the string on the umbrella) together. Hang the umbrellas with raindrops falling on them, and let students lift the flaps to see who is keeping dry.

Mud Puddle Pie

As the spring rain pours down, mud puddles pop up. Celebrate this spring phenomenon with a delicious mud pie. Makes one pie, approximately 10 servings.

Ingredients:
- 2 cups graham cracker crumbs
- ½ stick of butter, melted
- 1 package chocolate pudding, prepared according to box directions
- ½ cup chocolate cookie crumbs
  gummy worm-shaped candy (optional)

Mix the melted butter and graham cracker crumbs together until all crumbs are moist. Press the mixture into a 9" pie pan, sprayed lightly with non-stick spray. Freeze the pie pan for 30 minutes to set the crust. Then, spoon in the chocolate pudding. If desired, bury gummy worms in the pudding. Top the pie with chocolate cookie crumbs (dirt). Chill the pie for one hour, then serve.

Spring Cleaning

What would spring be without cleaning? Get a jump-start on classroom spring cleaning with some fun cleaning "games," such as wastepaper basket free throws, straighten or alphabetize bookshelf race, a neat desk contest, or a floor sweep relay. As students clean out desks and straighten bookshelves, let them have some fun and reward their hard work with a spring treat, like *Mud Puddle Pie* (above).

26

umbrella top
(also use with bulletin board idea, page 14)

COPY and
CUT

umbrella handle
(also use with bulletin board
idea, page 14)

raindrop
(also use with bulletin
board idea, page 14)

27

crocus pistil

crocus petals

COPY and CUT

bird
(also use with bulletin board idea,
page 14)

Women's History month began in 1978 when an Education Task Force in California initiated a Women's History Week highlighting women's accomplishments. They chose the week of March 8 to coincide with International Women's Day. The celebrations met with enthusiastic response. In 1981, the United States congress declared National Women's History Week and in 1987 expanded it to include the month of March.

Did You Know?

❈ In 1840, Esther Howland of Worcester, Massachusetts, invented mass-produced Valentines and patented the brown grocery bag.

❈ Between 1854 and 1860, during the Crimean War, Florence Nightingale revolutionized the nursing profession, decreasing soldiers' death rate from 60% to just 1%.

❈ In 1872, Susan B. Anthony was arrested for voting in a Presidential election. Women in the United States won the right to vote legally in 1920.

❈ In 1981, Sandra Day O'Connor became the first female United States Supreme Court Justice.

Literature Selections

America's Daughters: 400 Years of American Women by Judith Head: Perspective Publications, 1999. (Informational book, 128 pg.) Overview of women in American history from 1600 to the present. Includes many names left out of other sources.

Explorers (Women in Profile Series) by Carlotta Hacker: Crabtree Publishers, 1998. (Informational book, 48 pg.) Provides in-depth and numerous brief profiles of six 20th-century women who have made significant contributions to their fields. Other titles in the series include: *Musicians, Nobel Prize Winners, Political Leaders, Scientists, Writers*.

Girls Think of Everything: Stories of Ingenious Inventions by Women by Catherine Thimmesh: Houghton Mifflin Co., 2000. (Informational book, 64 pg.) Inventions of ten women and two girls are explored, from the most practical (windshield wipers) to the best loved (chocolate chip cookies).

Gallery of Famous Women

Create a women's history wall of fame in your classroom. Have each child choose a woman to profile. Students can choose from the women profiled in this chapter, from the *Women's History Matching Game* (page 36), or from other sources. Give each child a large sheet of white construction paper to fold in half. Have each student decorate the front of the paper as a portrait within a frame, then write a report on the inside. Put hook and loop dots on the inside edges so that the portraits will stay closed when hanging on the wall. Display the reports as a gallery of famous women. Have students make "velvet" rope barriers from construction paper to tape under the portraits to look like a gallery.

Sandra Day O'Connor

Court Justice and the first female member.

Sybil Ludington

Sybil Ludington (1761-1839), revolutionary war heroine, is the lesser known female counterpart to Paul Revere. Ludington, the oldest of eight children, was 16 on the evening of April 26, 1777 when the British began burning the town of Danbury, Connecticut—25 miles from her house. She was putting her siblings to bed when she received word of the British action. Her father was a colonel in the local militia. His troops were scattered over a wide area near her home in Fredericksburg, New York (now Ludington). She persuaded her father to let her summon the troops while he stayed at home to organize them as they arrived. On her horse, Star, she covered over 40 miles on dark, unmarked roads during a rainstorm—knocking on doors and crying "Turn back the Redcoats! Muster at Ludington's!" Thanks to her bravery, the troops drove the British back to their ships in Long Island Sound. Today, markers are placed along the route to show the path she took.

Explain the genre of historical fiction and the use of "creative license." Instruct students to write a short story about the ride of Sybil Ludington. Ask them to imagine her feelings during the journey, what she might have seen or heard, problems she might have encountered, and what her reaction might have been when she returned home at sunrise and learned that her father's militia had defeated the British.

Sacajawea (1788-1813?), a Shoshone Native American, acted as interpreter, guide, and peacemaker to the Lewis and Clark expedition (1804-1806). The purpose of the expedition was to find a water route to connect the Mississippi with the Pacific. Lewis and Clark hired Sacajawea's husband, not for his skills, but for hers. She showed the explorers how to find edible roots unknown to European-Americans. With her infant son bound to her back, she single-handedly rescued Captain Clark's journals from Missouri white water. Most importantly, Sacajawea and her infant served as a "white flag" of peace for the expedition. Sacajawea has been honored with statues and landmarks, and as the namesake of streams, lakes, parks, songs, and poems. Her image now appears on the United States golden dollar coin.

Sacajawea

Let students navigate their classmates to honor one of Sacajawea's contributions to the Lewis and Clark expedition. Pair students and let one be an explorer and the other a guide. Instruct the guides to choose objects in the room and verbally guide explorers to the objects using classroom landmarks, such as, "Now you will pass a mountain of books." If desired, allow students to guide each other around the playground. Label playground equipment with different landmarks (streams, mountains, etc.). Encourage students to switch roles and navigate to another location. After each partner has had a turn being both explorer and guide, talk about which role was easier and how Sacajawea may have felt navigating for Lewis and Clark.

men's History Month   Women's Histo

Sojourner Truth (1797?-1883) was a female abolitionist. Born into slavery with the name Isabell Baumfree, she escaped from her owner in New York after being sold and separated from her family. Baumfree had a strong faith in God and changed her name to Sojourner Truth because she believed she had been called by God to travel and talk to people about renouncing their sins. During the Civil War, she sang and preached the truth about slavery to make money for black soldiers serving in the Union army. She lived long enough to see the end of slavery, but never stopped speaking for racial and gender equality.

When Truth spoke, she wore a banner which read, "Proclaim liberty throughout the land unto all inhabitants thereof." Allow students to make banners to wear and "sojourn" from classroom to classroom spreading "truths" about Women's History. Provide butcher paper for students to make banners to wear in honor of Sojourner Truth. Children can decorate and write statements about "freedom" on the banners. Students can speak to each class about Sojourner Truth or other famous women they have studied during Women's History Month.

Sojourner Truth

Mary Cassatt

Mary Cassatt (1844-1926), a female Impressionist artist born in Pennsylvania, was the first American woman painter to win international acclaim. She studied at the Pennsylvania Academy of Fine Arts, then traveled to Paris to study with the Impressionists—a group of painters who were revolutionizing the art of painting with theories of light and color. Her unique work is characterized by bright colors, light, shadow, and the depictions of mothers and their children— an uncommon subject for artists of that period.

Show students examples of Cassatt's work and let them create Mary Cassatt-type drawings. Have students choose typical subject matter, such as someone showing care for another person. Use colored chalk on dark construction paper to create a drawing, then use tissues to blend the colors in an Impressionist style, working on one small section of the drawing at a time. Have students add details to the features after colors are blended.

Suzy and Rita

Juliet Gordon Low (1860-1927) was born into a wealthy family in Savannah, Georgia but did not enjoy behaving like a proper "Southern Belle." In 1912, she used her own money to start the first American Girl Scout troop. She began with 18 Savannah girls and developed programs to teach them skills that were traditionally associated with males, such as physical fitness, camping, and survival skills. By the end of her life, there were 167,000 Girl Scouts in the United States. Today, Girl Scouts of America has over 3 million members.

Juliet Gordon Low

Celebrate the Girl Scout tradition by asking local scout leaders or parent volunteers to come to class and teach skills such as first aid, sewing, knot tying, etc. Have each parent set up an instruction station. Allow students to visit the stations that interest them. Provide white paper circles on which students can design badges for the skills they have learned. Let students tape on the badges from each station they have visited. If desired, display the badges on student-made paper sashes which resemble the sashes worn by real Girl Scouts.

Marie Curie (1867-1934) was a Polish scientist who became famous for her work in physics and chemistry. She and her husband Pierre discovered two radioactive elements: radium and polonium. The couple shared the 1903 Nobel Prize for physics (the first for a woman) with Antoine Bacquerel. In 1911, Marie Curie won a second Nobel Prize for her study of radium which led to the invention of the X-ray. She also created mobile X-ray vans which traveled to patients, allowing them to remain motionless until help arrived.

If possible, ask a local hospital or doctor's office for X-rays to show to the class. Provide anatomy reference and point out the bones (especially broken bones) to see if students can identify them. Give each child a large sheet of paper (any color) and a smaller sheet of black paper. Have her draw a self-portrait on the colored paper. Then, let each student look at the skeletal reference and use white chalk to draw the bones from a section of her body on the black paper. Tape the "X-ray" over the self-portrait so that the two drawings line up. Make sure students label the bones they draw, then post your X-rays around the room.

Marie Curie

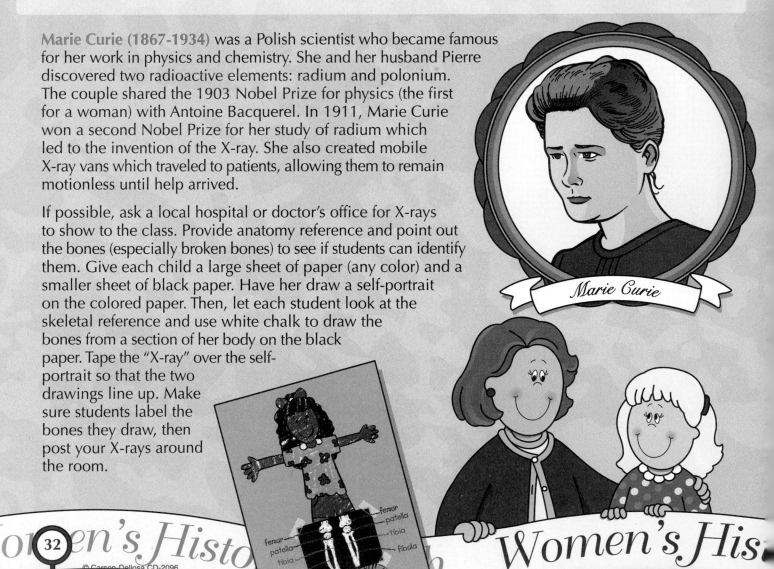

Eleanor Roosevelt (1884-1962) began a life of public service after her husband, President Franklin Roosevelt, developed polio. From that time forward she served as a political surrogate for him. She was committed to the rights of women, minorities, and the disadvantaged. After her husband's death, she served as a delegate to the newly established United Nations. She helped write the Universal Declaration of Human Rights which states: "All people are born free and equal in dignity and rights."

Eleanor Roosevelt was the first woman to have a syndicated column in American newspapers. Her *My Day* articles promoted the campaign for equal rights for women and minorities. Help students start a newspaper column. Let the class vote on a local issue which is important to them, such as cleaning up a creek or promoting school safety. Then, each time the school newspaper is published, have a few students prepare an article about a different aspect of the chosen topic. For example, if school safety is the topic, articles could address bus safety, hall safety, conflict resolution, etc. If your school does not have a newspaper, post the articles in the classroom or on a school bulletin board.

Eleanor Roosevelt

Mother Teresa (1910-1997) was born Agnes Gonxha (GON•ja) Bojaxhiu (boy•yah•JEE•yoo) in Albania (now Macedonia). In an interview she once said, "At the age of 12, I first knew I had a vocation to help the poor." She became a nun when she was 18 and in 1950 established the Congregation of Missionaries of Charity in India. It grew to over 3,000 sisters from several nations and they established more than 50 houses around the world to aid the poor. Mother Teresa received the Pope John XXIII Peace Prize in 1971 and the Nobel Peace Prize in 1979. She used the prize money to aid her charity work. She continued her work until the age of 87 when the world mourned her death.

Ask students to tell about times that they have helped others. How did it make them feel? Challenge students to vote on a slogan and create posters for a school fund-raiser which asks people to donate clothing, canned goods, old toys, etc. When the designated time for the fund-raiser has expired, let children pack the donations and send them to a local charity, such as a soup kitchen or the Red Cross.

Mother Teresa

Soup

Sow a Seed of kindness— SHARE!

KINDNESS

Canned Food Drive
Carter School
March 7th-21st

Ruth Handler

Ruth Handler (1916-) is a California entrepreneur who created the Barbie® doll and cofounded, with her husband Elliot, the toy company that became Mattel, Inc. Handler watched her daughter, Barbara, play with paper dolls, and noticed that she preferred teenage or adult paper dolls to cutouts of babies or children. Barbie® was introduced at the New York toy fair in 1959 and became an instant success. The doll is now available in 150 countries and sells at the rate of two dolls every second.

In the tradition of Ruth Handler, encourage children to invent a new, bestselling toy. Let students draw their inventions or use craft supplies to make models. When the toys are complete, have students present their new toys to the class, in hopes of "selling" the idea. Remind them to state the advantages of their new toys, why they would be good toys to own, etc. After all the toys have been presented, let students vote on which three toys their company will buy and begin to manufacture.

CAROL'S CRAZY CAR

Jane Goodall (1934-) is a British naturalist best known for her observations of chimpanzees in the wild. Twenty-three-year-old Goodall arrived in Kenya in 1957 to assist prominent anthropologist Louis Leakey in studying chimpanzees. She spent days trailing them through the forest and recording their habits. Her findings challenged the conventional ideas about the animals—that they were primitive apes living a simple existence. Goodall found them to be intelligent, emotional creatures that use tools and live in complex social groups.

Ask each student to choose an animal that he would want to observe in its habitat. Have each student research an animal and present his report in a file folder. On the cover he can draw a picture of himself with the animal and write the title "When I Lived with the _____." On the inside of the folder, he can compose a data sheet on the left side, noting the animal's name, diet, habitat, behavior, etc. The right side of the folder can contain an imaginary story about the time he spent with the animals.

Jane Goodall

When I Lived with the Raccoon

by Tony

Valentina Tereshkova (1937-), a Russian cosmonaut, was the first woman to travel in space. She withdrew from school and began working in a textile plant at age 16. Tereshkova continued her education through correspondence courses and began parachuting as a hobby. The Soviet space program selected her based on her parachuting skills. Code-named the Sea Gull, she piloted the 1963 Vostok 6 mission which remained in space for three days and orbited the Earth 48 times—once every 88 minutes. After the spacecraft reentered the Earth's atmosphere, Tereshkova parachuted to the ground as was typical of cosmonauts at that time.

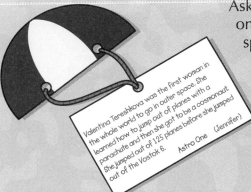

Valentina Tereshkova was the first woman in the whole world to go in outer space. She learned how to jump out of planes with a parachute and then she got to be a cosmonaut. She jumped out of 125 planes before she jumped out of the Vostok 6.　　Astro One　(Jennifer)

Valentina Tereshkova

Ask students to write reports on Tereshkova's life and space career. Students can use colorful construction paper to design parachutes from which to hang the reports. Attach the reports to construction paper and use yarn to suspend the reports from the parachutes. Ask students to sign their reports with their own names and to make up code names for themselves as if they were astronauts.

Wilma Rudolph (1940-1994) became an international hero when she became the first American woman to win three gold medals in a single Olympics (for 100-meter dash, 200-meter dash, and 400-meter relay). She was born in Tennessee, the 20th of 22 children. At the age of four, she was stricken with whooping cough, scarlet fever, double pneumonia, and polio, which caused her left leg to become withered and paralyzed. Doctors said she would never be able to walk, but she began to walk when she was nine years old and wore a brace until age 12. Her brothers and sisters took turns massaging her crippled leg and she eventually recovered enough to play high school basketball, run track at Tennessee State, and be named the "fastest woman in the world" in 1960.

Wilma Rudolph

Inform students that fans of Wilma Rudolph were told, "Don't blink. You might miss her." Wilma Rudolph could run 100 meters in 11 seconds. Mark off that distance outside and time each student while she runs. If desired, have all students run simultaneously in a 100-meter race. Compare the times to Rudolph's to see how fast she was.

Name _____

Women's History Matching Game

Read the clues and draw lines to match them to the names of famous women.

1. She became blind and deaf when she was about 19 months old. With the help of her teacher, Anne Sullivan, she graduated from college and became a spokeswoman for the disabled.

2. She served as Prime Minister of Israel from 1969-1974.

3. In 1983, she became the first American woman in space during her six-day flight on the space shuttle *Challenger*.

4. While owner of the Toll House Inn in Massachusetts, she invented the chocolate chip cookie.

5. She was the first woman to become a United States Supreme Court Justice.

6. She warned about the dangers of chemical pesticides to the environment in her book *The Silent Spring*.

7. Her book, *Little House in the Big Woods*, was about her childhood experiences on the frontier.

8. She was arrested for refusing to give up her seat on a bus to a white man and became known as the "mother of the civil rights movement."

9. Because of her antislavery novel, *Uncle Tom's Cabin*, Abraham Lincoln called her "the little lady who started a big war."

A. Rachel Carson

B. Sally Ride

C. Rosa Parks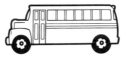

D. Sandra Day O'Connor

E. Hellen Keller

F. Harriet Beecher Stowe

G. Ruth Wakefield

H. Laura Ingalls Wilder

I. Golda Meir

Answers: 1. E 2. I 3. B 4. G 5. D 6. A 7. H 8. C 9. F

CATCH THE WIND

We cannot see the wind, but we know it is there! Students will be blown away by these easy, breezy facts and activities about the wind!

DID YOU KNOW?

- The world record for the highest wind gust (other than those associated with tornadoes) is held by the Mount Washington Observatory in New Hampshire. On April 12, 1934, a wind gust was measured at 231 miles per hour!
- Strong winds are present in all kinds of storms: dust storms, thunderstorms, hurricanes and typhoons, and tornadoes—the most violent winds of all!
- The Chinese probably invented the first kites sometime between 1000-400 B.C.
- Daniel Bernoulli (1700-1782), a Swiss scientist, discovered how air pressure helps birds fly.

LITERATURE SELECTIONS

Feel the Wind by Arthur Dorros: HarperCollins, 1989. (Picture book, 32 pg.) Explains why the wind blows and how it affects the world around us.

Gilberto and the Wind by Marie Hall Ets: Penguin Putnam Books for Young Readers, 1978. (Picture book, 32 pg.) For Gilberto, the wind is a fun and exciting playmate.

The Wind Blew by Pat Hutchens: Aladdin paperbacks, 1993. (Picture book, 32 pg.) A mischievous wind keep owners scrambling after their belongings.

Wind Says Good Night by Katy Rydell: Houghton Mifflin Co., 1994. (Picture book, 32 pg.) The friendly wind helps a child go to sleep.

FULL OF HOT AIR

The wind is full of hot air—and cold air, too! Air which has been heated by the sun rises, and then cooler air rushes in to fill the empty space. This movement of air creates wind. To demonstrate warm air rising, fill a small, glass soda bottle with ice water to cool the air inside. Pour out the water. Stretch a balloon over the opening of the cold, empty bottle. Place the bottle upright in a pan of hot water. The air under the balloon will absorb heat from the hot water, like air in the atmosphere absorbs heat from the sun. The hot air rises and expands the balloon. Ask students what will happen if they place the bottle in cold water (the cool air will sink into the bottle and contract, causing the balloon to deflate).

HEAR THE WIND BLOW

Sometimes the wind can be heard as well as seen and felt! Wind chimes indicate how fast and hard the wind is blowing. Ask students to bring in metal objects such as old keys, old flatware, washers, small bells, etc. Give each child two cardboard circles, each 4" in diameter (plastic canister lids also work). Punch a few holes around the edge of one circle. Tie a length of plastic filament through each hole, then tie the other end to a metal object. Punch a hole in the center of the circle and thread a 1' length of plastic filament through the hole. Tie the line around a paper clip to keep it from sliding back through the hole. Let students decorate the second circle, then attach it to the plastic filament (for wind resistance). Tie the wind chimes outside a classroom window, or send them home to be enjoyed.

SEE THE WIND

The invisible wind causes visible action! Make wind socks to show the wind. Give each child a large sheet of tissue paper and a pipe cleaner. Form the one end of the pipe cleaner into a 3" circle, and twist the remaining lengths together to form a handle. Roll one end of the tissue paper around the pipe cleaner and fold about 1" of the edge over the pipe cleaner. Secure the paper with tape. Cut the bottom third of the tissue paper into strips. Tie the wind socks outside of a classroom window, and watch them flutter!

FEEL THE WIND

Wind can caress your face, make you cold, or sting your eyes! Find out how wind makes students feel with wind poems. First, play "wind" music or a nature tape with wind sounds, or take students outside to experience the wind. Ask students to think about how the wind makes them feel. Then, have them write poems describing particular types of wind they are imagining, with the words in the shape of the wind. Give each student a large sheet of construction paper on which to copy her poem and add illustrations. Post the windy poems on a bulletin board titled *Feel the Wind Blow*.

I like the wind
That doesn't blow hard
It sways the flowers
In my yard.

It moves my hair
And flaps my dress
The warm spring wind
I like the best!

by Kelly H.

38

NORTH, SOUTH, EAST, WEST

Which direction is the wind blowing, and what difference does it make? Many people forecast the weather by observing the direction from which the wind is blowing. For example, in the United States, winter winds blowing from the east or north may bring snow. Strong winds blowing from the southwest may mean thunderstorms. Use this weather vane craft to determine wind direction. Give each student a paper plate and have her draw two perpendicular lines on it. Around the edges, label the lines north, south, east, and west. Make sure children put their labels in the correct positions. Give each child four 2' streamers to staple to the bottom of the plate, where the lines meet. Take the class outside and use a compass to find north. Instruct each student to face north and hold her plate parallel to the ground, pointing the north label toward north. Ask students which way the streamers are blowing. If the streamers are blowing toward the word *north*, then the wind is blowing from the south. If the streamers are blowing toward the word *east*, then the wind is blowing from the west. Measure the wind direction several times during the day. Does the wind change directions as it becomes later in the day?

WIND POWER

Harnessing the power of the wind has helped people use its energy to perform difficult tasks. *Windmills* have been used since ancient times to turn large stones to grind grain into flour, pump water from wells, and even drain water from flooded land. Have each student make a miniature windmill. Let each child cut out and color the windmill pattern (page 46) without cutting the center hole. Then, demonstrate how to bend the corner of each sail in the same direction so the wind will cause the sails to move. To make the base of the windmill, push a thumbtack through the center hole of the windmill pattern and into the upper part of a tall, plastic foam cup. Fill the cups with rocks to weigh them down, then let students take the windmills outside, stand in front of a fan, or produce their own wind by blowing into the sails.

HOW MUCH WIND IS WINDY?

Measuring wind is a breeze when using a wind measurement scale. Students can make their own hand-held references for wind speed. Explain that the *Beaufort Wind Scale* approximates wind speed by examining the relative movement of objects. Give each child a copy of the wind scale pattern (page 45) to cut out. Then, give each child two paper plates. Glue the wind scale pattern to the center of one plate, then top with the second plate. Cut a wedge from the second plate. Attach the two plates together in the center with a paper fastener. Let children go outside and examine trees, flags, etc., to determine how fast the wind is blowing by using their wind scales.

WIND SCALE

8-12 mph. Gentle breeze. Twigs move; light flags extend.

39

TURN-ME-OVER WIND BOOK

Most of the time, the wind is a pleasant breeze. However, anyone who has survived a strong thunderstorm, tornado, or hurricane knows that sometimes the wind can be harmful and dangerous! Explore these two aspects of wind with turn-me-over books! Give several sheets of paper to each student. Have him draw a cloud shape on one page, cut it out, then trace it on several other sheets of paper. Cut out the patterns, stack them, then staple the patterns together on the left side. On the top sheet, let each child draw a happy wind face. On the remaining right-hand pages, students should write and illustrate ways in which the wind is helpful, such as *Wind helps me fly a kite,* or *Wind helps people sail boats.* Have each student flip over the book so that the back page is the cover, illustrate an angry wind face, and write the title *Wind Can be Harmful.* On the right-hand pages, have students write and illustrate ways in which the wind can be harmful, such as *Wind can make windows break,* or *Wind can blow down trees.* Place the turn-me-over books in a science center or have children share them aloud.

WIND CAN BE HELPFUL

Front

WIND CAN BE HARMFUL

Back

"WIND-FORMATION"

The answers to these questions are blowing in the wind...literally! Provide resources about wind storms, such as hurricanes, blizzards, tornadoes, etc. Assign students to groups and give each group a copy of the *Find it in the Wind* worksheet (page 46) with the answer key removed. (This scavenger hunt worksheet makes a great Internet search project!) Reward the first group to find all the answers with a wind-related prize, such as a pinwheel.

BIG WINDS AND AIR PRESSURE

Tornadoes take the cake—or blow it away, rather, when it comes to violent wind. Tornadoes can contain wind speeds of up to 300 miles per hour. Demonstrate the movement of wind in a tornado with a "bottled tornado." Fill a two-liter, plastic soda bottle with water. Over a sink or outside, turn the bottle upside down and let it "chug" out of the opening. Then, refill the bottle and pour it out again, but this time swirl the bottle in a counterclockwise direction. The water should form a vortex in the bottle and pour out much more quickly.

FLYING MACHINES

Now that students know a little about wind, they can put that knowledge to work with these fun flying machines and wind toys!

UP, UP, AND AWAY!

Capture students' fancy with hot air balloons! These flying machines were invented by Joseph and Étienne Montgolfier in France, and were first launched in 1783. Explain that balloons fly because they contain either helium or heated air, which makes them lighter than the surrounding air. Let each student design his own balloon. Provide books or search the Internet for color photographs of balloons (most balloons have unique designs). Give each child a white paper lunch bag, and have him decorate it on all sides using paint, markers, crayons, etc. Stuff the bag with shredded newspaper, then wrap a rubber band around the bottom. Provide a plastic berry basket for each child to attach to the balloon using four strands of yarn. Poke an unfolded paper clip in the top of each balloon and tie a length of string to the paper clip. Hang all the balloons from the classroom ceiling for students to enjoy.

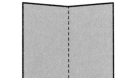
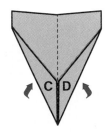

AIRPLANE AERODYNAMICS

Take airplane fun to greater heights with a paper plane air show. To prepare for the air show, give each child a sheet of paper and have him follow the paper airplane-folding instructions below. Then, let students write their names on their planes. Before taking students outside to send their planes soaring, explain that when Ohio natives Orville and Wilber Wright invented the first powered airplane, which they flew on December 3, 1903, at Kitty Hawk, NC, their flight lasted 12 seconds and only flew 120 feet. Have students measure the distances of their plane flights. Allow them to experiment with different folding techniques and try to make their planes fly farther.

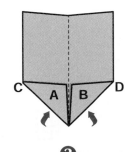

❶ Fold a letter-sized sheet of paper in half lengthwise, then unfold the paper.

❷ Fold A and B into the center of the paper.

❸ Fold C and D into the center of the paper.

❹ Fold the plane in half again.

❺ Fold down the wings evenly.

41

HAPPY HELICOPTERS

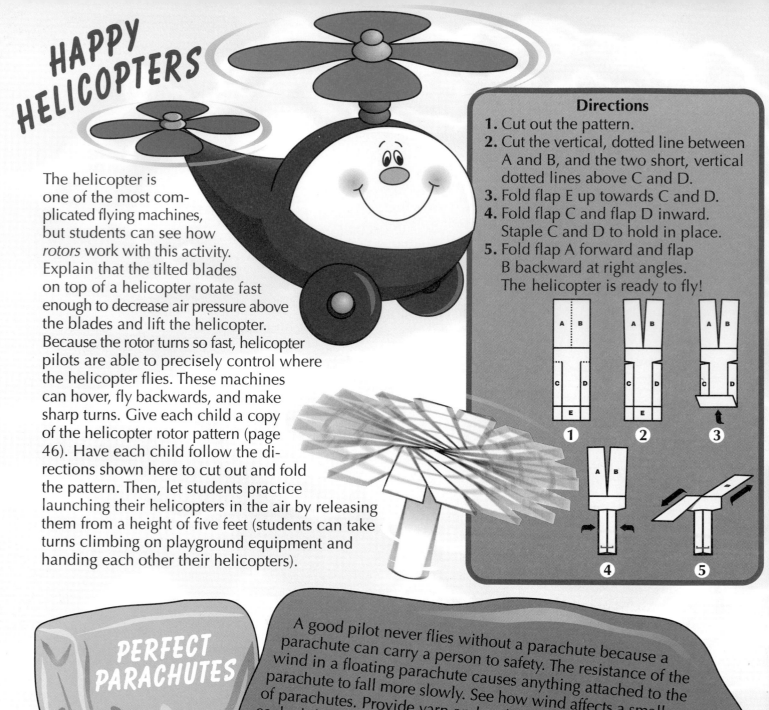

The helicopter is one of the most complicated flying machines, but students can see how *rotors* work with this activity. Explain that the tilted blades on top of a helicopter rotate fast enough to decrease air pressure above the blades and lift the helicopter. Because the rotor turns so fast, helicopter pilots are able to precisely control where the helicopter flies. These machines can hover, fly backwards, and make sharp turns. Give each child a copy of the helicopter rotor pattern (page 46). Have each child follow the directions shown here to cut out and fold the pattern. Then, let students practice launching their helicopters in the air by releasing them from a height of five feet (students can take turns climbing on playground equipment and handing each other their helicopters).

Directions

1. Cut out the pattern.
2. Cut the vertical, dotted line between A and B, and the two short, vertical dotted lines above C and D.
3. Fold flap E up towards C and D.
4. Fold flap C and flap D inward. Staple C and D to hold in place.
5. Fold flap A forward and flap B backward at right angles. The helicopter is ready to fly!

PERFECT PARACHUTES

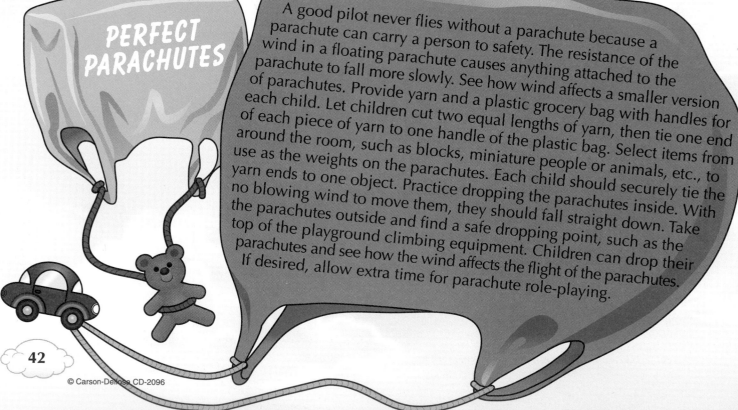

A good pilot never flies without a parachute because a parachute can carry a person to safety. The resistance of the wind in a floating parachute causes anything attached to the parachute to fall more slowly. See how wind affects a smaller version of parachutes. Provide yarn and a plastic grocery bag with handles for each child. Let children cut two equal lengths of yarn, then tie one end of each piece of yarn to one handle of the plastic bag. Select items from around the room, such as blocks, miniature people or animals, etc., to use as the weights on the parachutes. Each child should securely tie the yarn ends to one object. Practice dropping the parachutes inside. With no blowing wind to move them, they should fall straight down. Take the parachutes outside and find a safe dropping point, such as the top of the playground climbing equipment. Children can drop their parachutes and see how the wind affects the flight of the parachutes. If desired, allow extra time for parachute role-playing.

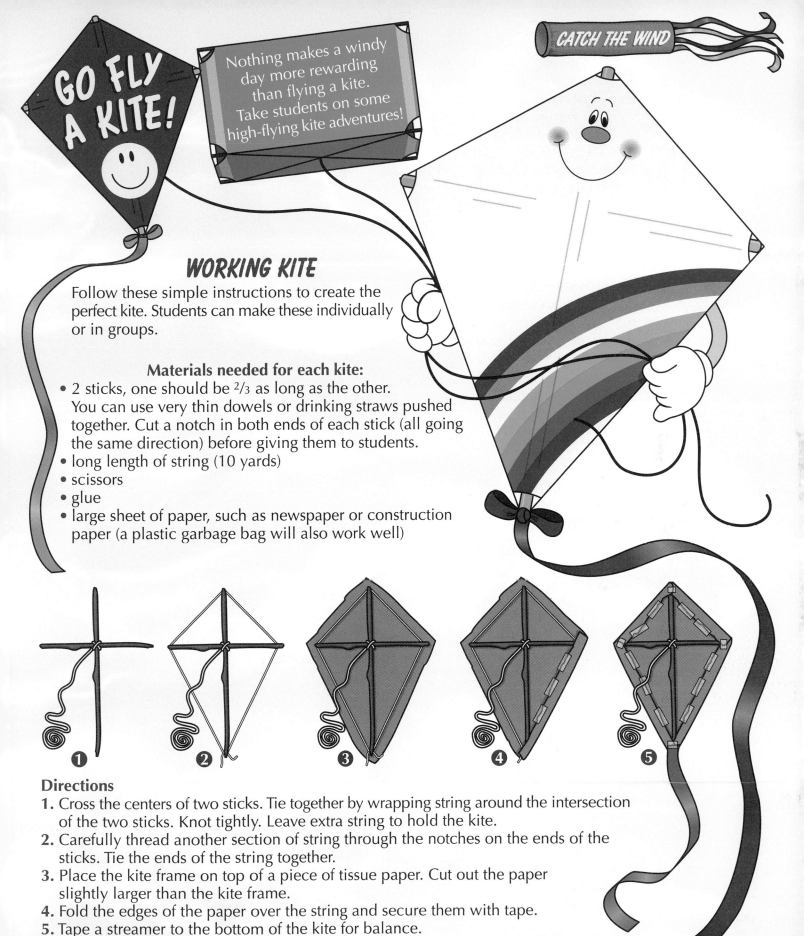

GO FLY A KITE!

Nothing makes a windy day more rewarding than flying a kite. Take students on some high-flying kite adventures!

CATCH THE WIND

WORKING KITE

Follow these simple instructions to create the perfect kite. Students can make these individually or in groups.

Materials needed for each kite:

- 2 sticks, one should be ²/₃ as long as the other. You can use very thin dowels or drinking straws pushed together. Cut a notch in both ends of each stick (all going the same direction) before giving them to students.
- long length of string (10 yards)
- scissors
- glue
- large sheet of paper, such as newspaper or construction paper (a plastic garbage bag will also work well)

❶ ❷ ❸ ❹ ❺

Directions

1. Cross the centers of two sticks. Tie together by wrapping string around the intersection of the two sticks. Knot tightly. Leave extra string to hold the kite.
2. Carefully thread another section of string through the notches on the ends of the sticks. Tie the ends of the string together.
3. Place the kite frame on top of a piece of tissue paper. Cut out the paper slightly larger than the kite frame.
4. Fold the edges of the paper over the string and secure them with tape.
5. Tape a streamer to the bottom of the kite for balance.

*Complete the **Kite Safety** worksheet (page 47) by adding pictures to the text in each section of the worksheet.*

On the kite illustration:

Once upon a time, a boy named Karl bought a kite. He named it Kit. He flew Kit very high, but Kit got stuck in a tree. Oh no! Karl was sad, but then a big kid named Kevin came along. Karl was scared.

On the bows (string):

"I want to help," said Kevin. He went up into the tree.

Kevin took Kit out of the tree.

He gave Kit back to Karl and smiled. Karl was happy.

They flew Kit together for the rest of the day.

KITE TALES

Kites are sure to inspire imaginative adventure stories from your students! Ask each student to write a rough draft of a kite adventure story. Have each student cut out a large, diamond kite shape from construction paper, and write some of his story on the kite, adding a small illustration if there is space. To finish the story, let each child cut out several bow patterns (page 47) from construction paper, and write the last few lines of the story on the bows. Staple a string to the bottom of the kite and tape the bows to the string. Post the colorful kite "tales" around the classroom.

KITE SNACK

Continue the high flying kite fun with tasty kite snacks. Give each student a paper plate with a square graham cracker, a licorice whip, small jelly beans, and miniature marshmallows. Instruct her to rotate the cracker so it is diamond-shaped. Spread the cracker with cream cheese or peanut butter and add jelly bean decorations. Press the licorice "tail" into the cream cheese on the bottom of the "kite," and top the kite tail with miniature marshmallows, pinched in the middle to represent bows.

MANY KITES— WHAT A SIGHT!

Although diamond-shaped kites are most commonly seen, there are many types of kites. Assign different kite designs, such as a box kite, compound, parafoil, delta, tetrahedron, fighting kite, etc. for small groups to research. Provide kite books and allow time for research so that each group can see pictures and learn about the history and design of its kite. Each group can write interesting facts about its kite, illustrate or build a model of it, then present the information to the class. If desired, have older students attempt to fly their models.

TETRAHEDRON KITE

The tetrahedron kite was invented by Alexander Graham Bell, the man who invented the telephone. The kites are linked together. Tetrahedron [made of very light] [like] straw and tissue paper, [Bell.]

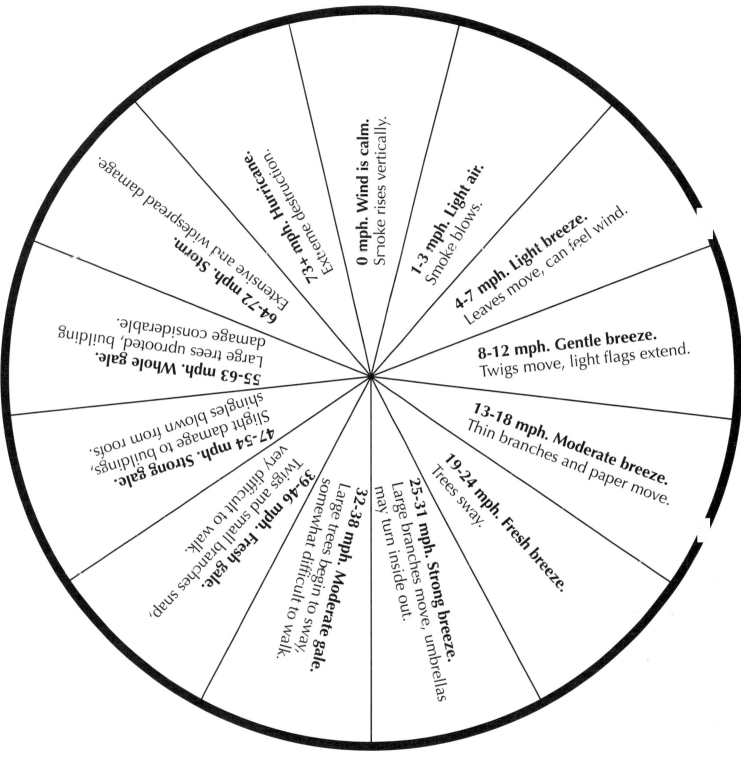

0 mph. Wind is calm. Smoke rises vertically.

1-3 mph. Light air. Smoke blows.

4-7 mph. Light breeze. Leaves move, can feel wind.

8-12 mph. Gentle breeze. Twigs move, light flags extend.

13-18 mph. Moderate breeze. Thin branches and paper move.

19-24 mph. Fresh breeze. Trees sway.

25-31 mph. Strong breeze. Large branches move, umbrellas may turn inside out.

32-38 mph. Moderate gale. Large trees begin to sway, somewhat difficult to walk.

39-46 mph. Fresh gale. Twigs and small branches snap, very difficult to walk.

47-54 mph. Strong gale. Slight damage to buildings, shingles blown from roofs.

55-63 mph. Whole gale. Large trees uprooted, building damage considerable.

64-72 mph. Storm. Extensive and widespread damage.

73+ mph. Hurricane. Extreme destruction.

wind scale

COPY and CUT

Find it in the Wind

On a separate sheet of paper, use any resources you can think of to answer these wind questions!

1 Who invented the first airplane?

2 What is another name for a hurricane that occurs in the Pacific Ocean?

3 How fast does the wind have to blow for a snowstorm to be called a blizzard?

4 What is a nickname for a tornado?

5 What is the difference between a storm watch and a storm warning?

6 Name two things a windmill can do.

- -

• ANSWER KEY •

1. Orville and Wilbur Wright
2. Typhoon
3. 32 mph
4. Twister, cyclone
5. A watch means that conditions are favorable for a storm. A warning means that a storm has been sighted by a spotter or on radar.
6. Grind corn, wheat, or other grain into flour, pump water from wells, generate electricity, pump out floodwaters.

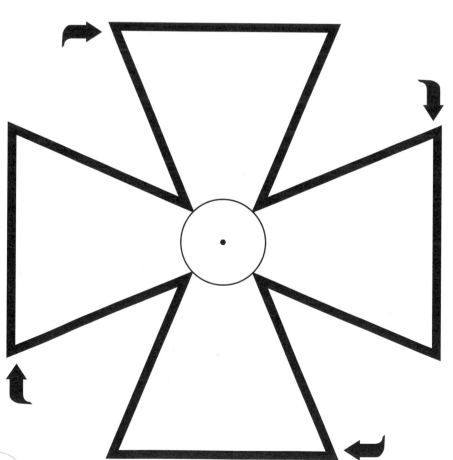

windmill

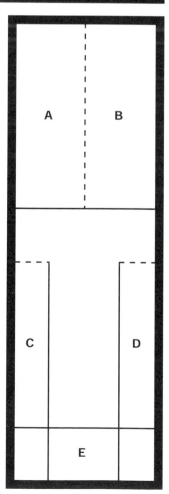

helicopter rotor

Students should add pictures to the text in each section of the kite. Then, cut out the kite.

Kite Safety

1. Fly kites in open areas, away from cars and groups of people.

2. Do not fly kites when the weather is stormy.

3. Do not fly kites near power lines.

4. Check the ground for holes, sticks, and rocks before you fly your kite.

bow

bow

47

NEWSPAPERS IN EDUCATION

Friday, March 25, 2005   Vol. XVIII   50 CENTS

Read All About Them!

During Newspapers in Education Week, celebrated the first week of March, treat your class to an "Extra! Extra!" fun and informative unit on newspapers!

PHOTO BY SAMANTHA MANCILL

Did You Know?

- In 59 B.C., Romans read the earliest known daily news sheet: the *Acta Diurna* (Daily Events).

- The printed word did not become widely available until the mid-1400s, when Johann Gutenberg invented moveable type.

- The first American newspaper, *Publick Occurrences Both Foreign and Domestic*, was published in 1690 by Benjamin Harris.

Literature Selections

Deadline! From News to Newspaper by Gail Gibbons: Ty Crowell Co., 1987. (Informational book, 32 pg.) Follows a typical day at a small daily paper.

The Furry News: How to Make a Newspaper by Loreen Leedy: Holiday House, 1990. (Picture book, 32 pg.) Defines newspaper terms and gives instructions for how to make a newspaper.

More Than Just News!

Few people read the entire newspaper each day. All of the information may seem especially overwhelming to beginning readers. Introduce students to some of the functions of a newspaper by examining it in specific parts. Assign students to groups and give each a different section of the newspaper, such as the classifieds, food section, international section, sports section, etc. Have each group complete specific tasks for its section, using the newspaper to cut out relevant information (see examples below). Let each group act as a team of reporters and tell what they found in their research, then post the articles and information on a bulletin board.

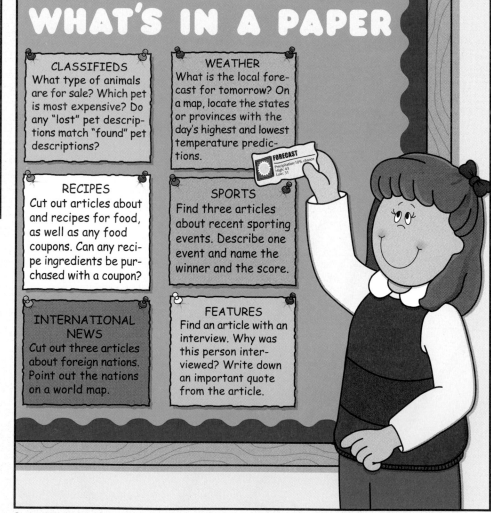

WHAT'S IN A PAPER

CLASSIFIEDS
What type of animals are for sale? Which pet is most expensive? Do any "lost" pet descriptions match "found" pet descriptions?

WEATHER
What is the local forecast for tomorrow? On a map, locate the states or provinces with the day's highest and lowest temperature predictions.

RECIPES
Cut out articles about and recipes for food, as well as any food coupons. Can any recipe ingredients be purchased with a coupon?

SPORTS
Find three articles about recent sporting events. Describe one event and name the winner and the score.

INTERNATIONAL NEWS
Cut out three articles about foreign nations. Point out the nations on a world map.

FEATURES
Find an article with an interview. Why was this person interviewed? Write down an important quote from the article.

FORECAST
Precipitation:10% chance
High: 45
Low: 31

Susan Wood matches her information from the local forecast section to the "What's in a Paper" Bulletin Board.

Newspaper Parts

To help readers navigate through the articles, newspapers use pictures and captions, exciting headlines, bylines—all of which make terrific pre-reading material! Ask students to work with partners. Give each pair a copy of the same article with each component (article, picture, headline, etc.) cut apart. Ask the pairs to glue the parts on a sheet of paper in the approximate places where they should appear. Have pairs label the parts as they glue them to the paper, then compare their notes with the original, uncut teacher's copy.

banner headline

Animals get boost from volunteers

headline

PHOTO BY MIKE SMITH

photo byline

8-year-old David Knight brings his foster puppy, Oscar, back to the shelter—just long enough to sign the adoption papers!

cutline

Local shelter gets much needed face-lift

Daily News Staff Report ← byline

The Lakeside Animal Shelter is a popular place to visit. The shelter, which holds homeless animals until they are adopted by new owners, hosts a weekly visitation session every Saturday during which people of all ages are encouraged to drop by and pet the 150 animals housed in the shelter. Will Neville, current head of operations, stated that, "After hearing all of our visitors talk about how much the shelter needed fixing up, I decided that anyone who cares about animals might be willing to help."

After distributing 200 fliers and calling people who had formerly adopted animals from the shelter, Mr. Neville found 77 volunteers willing to help out for the day, plus 35 people who gave foster care to the shelter's resident animals for the weekend. Pam Carter, adoptee of Gidget the Jack Russel terrier mix, said, "After the shelter took such good care of our dog before we got her, it seemed like the least we could do." Mrs. Carter took in five dogs over the weekend, including a 100-lb. Boxer named Buster. The foster animals were taken back to the shelter on Monday.

Volunteers helped deep-clean cages, wash windows, paint the inside and the outside of the building, replace air filters, make minor

(See Shelter, p. B5)

article

jump

Newspaper Terms

What's a *typo*? How about a *byline*? The newspaper industry is full of jargon. To familiarize students with important newspaper terms, let them complete the Jargon Jumble worksheet (page 52). Students can cut out an example of each word after they have completed the worksheet, glue them to a separate sheet of paper, and write each term next to its example word.

Headline Saves the Day!

Just as a good book title can convince someone to read a book, an attention-grabbing headline goes a long way to persuade someone to read an article. Explain that since most people do not read the entire newspaper, it is important for headlines to be clear and interesting. Have students read headlines from several newspapers. Talk about which headlines are most interesting and why. Let students make up their own creative headlines about school or class events. Read the headlines to the class, then let each child choose one and write a news story about it. Students who write about similar topics can compare their completed stories.

49

Guess What's Next?

Comic strips are terrific story sequencing material because you must wait to see what happens next! Choose an age-appropriate comic strip which has a continuing storyline. Each day for at least a week, cut out the strip and post it. Have students take turns reading the strip and making predictions about what will happen the next day. When you have read enough of the strip for the class to be familiar with the characters and the action, have each child draw her own version of the next day's strip, complete with panels and speech bubbles. Post the kid-drawn comic strips on a bulletin board beside the actual newspaper comic strips.

STAR EXPLORERS

Divide and Conquer

It takes many people to make a newspaper! Familiarize students with the steps involved and the people who work on the paper. Brainstorm a list of people who work on a newspaper (editors, writers/reporters, photographers, artists, advertising salespeople, typesetters, press operators, computer technicians, paper deliverers, etc.). If desired, brainstorm a list of the different kinds of beat reporters who specialize in one area, such as weather, food, international news, feature stories, advice column, etc. Then, let each student choose a different job title and research what that person does to help produce the newspaper. When students have completed their research, give them actual classified advertisements to use as models, and have students write classified advertisements for the positions they have researched.

Wayne Kirkland tries to fill a vacancy in the photography department.

Question Words in Action

Good news stories answer the question words: *who, what, where, when, how,* and *why*. Let students cut out and read short articles and determine whether these questions are answered in them. Post the Question Words Key (page 52). Have students write the question words around the articles, then draw arrows to the places in the text where the questions are answered. Post the articles and the Question Words Key for students to read.

What's Your Opinion?

Newspaper editorials provide readers with a forum for expressing and reading opinions. Use editorials to examine the role of opinions in writing. Discuss with the class what the word *opinion* means. Provide several appropriate editorial columns and letters to the editor for students to read and discuss. What are the topics of the letters and editorials? How do the writers express their opinions? How is an editorial different from a letter to the editor? Let students choose topics, such as field trips, lunchroom food, school visitors, etc., about which they would like to write editorial columns. Post the columns on a bulletin board, and let students each choose one letter to which they would like to respond with a letter to the editor. Post the responses beside the editorials.

PHOTO BY BRITANY WILSON

Just the Facts

What makes good news? Interesting and important events, of course! After students have completed the *Question Words in Action* activity (page 50), they are ready to choose a topic on which to report. Explain that the job of a reporter is to observe and record information: just the facts. Allow students to read several hard news stories. Then, brainstorm a list of events and situations that are happening around the school. Is a new building being constructed? Is there a class trip or field day scheduled? Assign a group to cover each newsworthy event. Let the groups decide which roles group members will play and at what time. Ideally, each student will get a chance to interview, write, and edit. Use the calendar grid (page 6) to schedule deadlines for interviewing, writing, editing, and completing artwork. When the groups have completed their reports, publish them on a bulletin board or in the classroom paper.

School Visitors
We have had some good visitors like a police officer and a writer, but we have not had a movie star. ...d like to see ...l movie sta...

PHOTO BY BLAKE THOMAS

Classroom Newspaper

As students become familiar with the form and function of newspapers, they may be eager to publish their own! To make the most of their interest, have each child write an article and "photograph" (illustrate) her story. (Students may wish to interview each other or friends and family members.) Post 11" x 17" sheets of paper vertically on a bulletin board so that students can paste up, or mock up, their stories by taping them to the paper. Encourage students to choose different types of stories so that there will be a variety. Have a contest to name the class paper, then copy the mock ups, fold them in half like newspapers, and distribute them to the class.

CLASS NEWS

Mrs. Thayer's Class

Rm. 402

Susan Davies Finds Family of Kittens

New Toy Store in Mall Has Great Selection!

School Picnic Rained Out

Kennedy Elementary Students Write New School Song

1. **Who** did the action in this article? Draw a red line under your answer.

2. **What** was the action? Draw a blue line under your answer.

3. **Where** was the action? Draw a green line under your answer.

4. **When** was the action? Draw a purple line under your answer.

5. **Why** did the action occur? Draw an orange line under your answer.

6. **How** did the action occur? Draw a black line under your answer.

- -

Jargon Jumble

Name _____

Directions: Using the jumbled words as clues, write each word from the word bank below on the line next to its matching definition

1. oopht = picture in a newspaper article _____

2. pumj = the point at which a story is continued on another page _____

3. leadhein = title of an article, usually in large, bold letters _____

4. linbye = small type that tells the source of a photograph _____

5. utcelin = caption under a photo _____

6. erticla = news or feature story _____

Word Bank					
headline	cutline	jump	byline	article	photo

Read with Dr. Seuss

Born on March 2, 1904, Theodor Seuss Geisel, better known as Dr. Seuss, wrote and illustrated 48 children's books during his lifetime. Dr. Seuss was asked by his publisher to write funny, imaginative books for beginning readers. He helped countless children learn to enjoy reading and was awarded a Pulitzer Prize in 1984. Celebrate his contribution to children's literature with these activities.

Did You Know?

- Dr. Seuss sometimes wrote under the name Theo LeSieg, which is his last name, Geisel, spelled backwards.
- The book *Green Eggs and Ham* was written on a bet. A friend bet Dr. Seuss fifty dollars that he could not write a book using just fifty simple words.
- The Grinch was Dr. Seuss's favorite book character.

Literature Selections

Oh, the Places He Went
by Maryann N. Weidt: Carolrhoda Books, Inc., 1994. (Biography, 64 pg.) Comprehensive biography for young readers provides facts and background information about some of Dr. Seuss's most famous children's books.

The Sneetches and Other Stories
by Theodor Seuss Geisel: Random House, 1988. (Picture Book, 64 pg.) A collection of four modern fables for students who cannot get enough of Dr. Seuss!

Famous Characters, New Stories

The Cat in the Hat, Horton the Elephant, The Grinch, and many other Dr. Seuss characters are loved by children. Use these characters to prompt creative writing. Let each child choose a character from a Dr. Seuss story, then write his own story featuring the character. Students can design book covers and make up titles for their stories. Add these one-of-a-kind stories to the classroom library for students to share.

53

The Foot Book
(Random House Children's Publishing, 1968)

Students can put their best feet forward with this funny foot activity. Tape a large piece of white butcher paper to a wall. Let students take turns drawing and coloring different pairs of animal feet. When the mural is complete, look at it with the class and let students name the feet they see. Then, label each pair of feet and read the words aloud as a class.

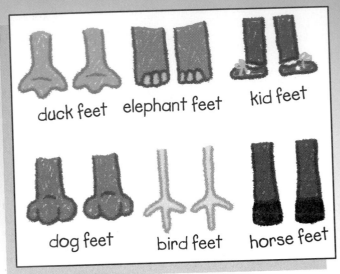

There's a Strock on top of the Clock

There's a Wocket in My Pocket!
(Random House Children's Publishing, 1974)

Learning household words has never been more fun! As students spot the hidden characters on each page, they learn words such as *shelf*, *bookcase*, *clock*, and *lamp*. After sharing the story, brainstorm a list of classroom objects. Let students choose words from the list, then write their own rhymes complete with unusual characters. Bind the rhymes into a class book. Encourage each student to illustrate the character featured in her rhyme. Let students post their characters in the appropriate places around the room. Read the class book aloud and let students locate and name the characters described in each rhyme.

Hop on Pop
(Random House Children's Publishing, 1963)

Perfect for beginning readers, this book features simple sentences with rhyming words. Encourage students to identify rhyming word patterns with this word chain activity. Have students sit in a circle. Say a word from the book, then go around the circle and have each child name a word that rhymes with the chosen word. As students say the words, list them on the board. When one word chain is complete, say another word and continue around the circle. Let students use the words to write and illustrate sentences similar to those in the book.

mop drop
I will drop the mop.

cake bake
We bake the cake.

fat cat
That cat is fat!

Dr. Seuss

Dr. Seuss's Sleep Book
(Random House Children's Publishing, 1962)

What makes you sleepy? Probably this bedtime story. Share the book at the end of the day, then have children think about what makes them sleepy. Make "sleepyhead" pictures by having each child draw and cut out an oval shape to represent a yawning mouth. Glue the shape in the center of a sheet of paper. Have each student draw a picture of himself around the oval. Below each picture, encourage students to write things that make them feel sleepy.

Warm cocoa makes me sleepy.

If I Ran the Zoo
(Random House Children's Publishing, 1950)

Filled with imaginative and exotic animals, this story is sure to spark an interest in the zoo. Have students work in groups of three to create pretend zoo animals. Give each group a sheet of 8 1/2" x 11" paper turned vertically and folded into thirds. Unfold the paper and have one child draw the animal's head in the top section. Fold the paper to cover the drawing and pass it to the second student to draw the animal's body in the middle section. Fold to cover this illustration and have the third child draw the animal's feet in the final section. Reveal the new zoo animal by unfolding the paper. Then, have the groups name their animals. Let students draw zoo habitats for their animals on construction paper. Have groups make signs with the names of the zoo animals. Display the creations on a wall or bulletin board.

bizantis

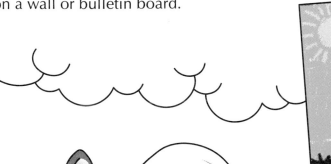

h at

c

The Cat in the Hat
(Random House Children's Publishing, 1957)

This classic story is the perfect teaching tool for word families. Copy, color, and cut out the hat pattern and word strip (page 59). Cut out a square space on the hat pattern. Next to the cut-out section, program the hat pattern with a word ending. Program the word strip with beginning letters and slide it through the slits. Have students slide the word strip to read the words made by combining beginning letters with the word ending. Make several different word family hats and store them in a center.

The Shape of Me and Other Stuff
(Random House Children's Publishing, 1973)

This Dr. Seuss book should shape-up to be a class favorite. As you read the story, encourage students to name the silhouettes and shapes they see. Ask each child to think of an object and draw it on black paper using a white, silver, or yellow crayon. Have students cut out the shape outlines, tape the tops to white paper, trace them, then lift the silhouettes and draw the real objects underneath. Post the pictures around the room so students can guess the objects, then lift the silhouettes to check their answers.

Green Eggs and Ham
(Random House Children's Publishing, 1960)

Do you like blue potatoes and gravy? Plaid bacon and eggs? Use this persuasive story to inspire students to think of food combinations that sound unappealing or unappetizing. Have each student illustrate her concoction, then write several sentences convincing others to try it. Display each different food combination and determine how many students would sample it by taking a class poll. If desired, share a simple snack with the class, such as pink cookies and milk (use strawberry powder or red food coloring).

Daisy-Head Mayzie
(Random House Children's Publishing, 1995, published posthumously)

Don't look now—you have a class full of Daisy-Head Mayzies! Have students make and wear special daisy headbands. Create a poster board strip about 3" wide to fit each student's head. Let each student draw, color, and cut out daisies from heavy paper and attach them to the top edge of the strip. Then, allow students to personalize their headbands. Encourage each child to write about how he would remove the daisy from his head if he were the character in the story.

Fox in Socks
(Random House Children's Publishing, 1965)

The funny alliterations in this book are sure to make tongues numb, as the last page promises. Use the text to inspire children to create tongue twisters. Divide the class into small groups, assign each group a letter, and have them brainstorm words beginning with that letter. Post the word lists around the room for students to use to write tricky tongue twisters. Let students exchange their tongue twisters with classmates to read aloud.

One Fish Two Fish Red Fish Blue Fish
(Random House Children's Publishing, 1960)

Striped fish, spotted fish, green fish, purple fish—see how many kinds of fish students can create. Copy a fish pattern (page 59) for each student. Allow students to decorate their patterns any way they wish, then cut out the fish. Cover a bulletin board with blue paper and attach the fish to it. Let students write sentences like those in the story to describe the fish on index cards, then attach the index cards near the fish they describe. For extra fun, design and add aquarium rocks, underwater plants, etc., on construction paper—Dr. Seuss style!

This fish is green.

This fish is red.

This fish is live.

This fish is dead.

If I Ran the Circus
(Random House, 1956)

Turn your classroom into a three-ring circus for students to run! Divide the class into small groups and challenge each to come up with a unique trick to perform. If desired, provide balls, hoops, bean bags, etc., for students to use. Allow the groups to practice their tricks. On circus day, use masking tape to divide the floor into three rings, then let the groups take turns performing their tricks in different rings.

Horton Hatches the Egg
(Random House Children's Publishing, 1940)

When a mother bird wants to leave her nest, she asks Horton, an elephant, to sit on her egg and protect it while she is gone. Horton keeps his promise and stays with the egg until it hatches. Have students think about the qualities Horton had that made him a good choice to stay with the egg. Then, provide a few egg patterns (page 59) for students to trace, and have them cut two egg shapes from construction paper. On one shape, let students write about Horton and his good qualities. Instruct students to color the other pattern, then cut it in half. Put the cut pattern on top of the writing page and attach the sides together at one edge with a paper fastener. "Hatch" each egg to read about Horton.

The Lorax **(Random House Children's Publishing,**

Through bright illustrations and a character who speaks on behalf of trees, this story teaches the importance of caring for the environment. Let students illustrate their own characters that speak for different parts of the environment, such as wildlife, rivers, soil, or oceans. Have students draw speech bubbles with advice from the characters on how to save this part of the environment. Hold a class environmental "forum" and allow students to present their advice.

I am the Jotax. Rivers can't talk, so I'm going to tell you how to save them. Stop throwing garbage and waste from factories into rivers. It kills the animals that live in the water and makes the water unsafe for people to drink.

And to Think That I Saw It on Mulberry Street
(Random House Children's Publishing, 1937)

Imagination runs wild in Dr. Seuss's first book about what a boy sees on his way to school. After he sees a wagon being pulled by a horse, the boy adds to and embellishes a story until it becomes unbelievable. Have your class work together to tell their own tall tale. Let the students sit in a circle. Begin the story by choosing a volunteer to name something he or she "saw" on the way to school and draw it on a large sheet of butcher paper posted on a wall. Move around the circle, letting each child add make-believe details to the story and to the picture until you have a truly outlandish tale!

word strip

hat

fish

egg

59

© Carson-Dellosa CD-2096

Celebrating Deaf History

Deaf History Month falls between March 13th and April 15th each year. It commemorates some important dates in deaf history, such as the opening of the first public school for the deaf (April 15, 1812), the date on which deaf students were allowed to earn college degrees (April 8, 1864), and the election of the first deaf president of Gallaudet University, a school for the deaf (March 13, 1988). This unit will help students learn the many ways in which deaf people communicate with each other and with the hearing.

Did You Know?

Most spoken languages have their own sign language. The same sign may represent different words in different languages.

Some deaf people have dogs that hear for them. The dogs are rescued from shelters and are trained to let their owners know when the phone or doorbell rings.

Some deaf musicians use their feet and hands to feel instrument vibrations. They can tell what note is being played from the frequency of the vibration.

Literature Selections

Moses Goes to a Concert by Isaac Millman: Farrar Straus & Giroux, 1998. (Picture book, 37 pg.) A young deaf boy goes to a concert on a school trip. Students learn to differentiate different sounds by holding balloons in their laps and feeling the vibrations.

Handsigns by Kathleen Fain: Chronicle Books, 1993. (Picture book, 40 pg.) Presents the American Manual Alphabet and an introductory history of American Sign Language.

Classroom As"sign"ment

Sign up students for an experience sure to immerse them in deaf culture by teaching them some of the ways deaf people communicate. Explain that Gallaudet University, founded in 1817 in Washington, D.C., was named for its founder Thomas Hopkins Gallaudet and was the first United States university for deaf students. Some schools for deaf students have classes that teach only in sign language, while others have classes in which students must read their teachers' lips. Brainstorm a list of short words with students, then finger spell the words. Have students guess which word you are spelling. Next, try the exercise by mouthing the words. Which method do students prefer?

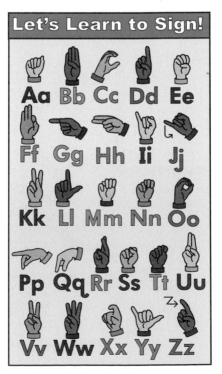

Let's Learn to Sign!

Aa Bb Cc Dd Ee
Ff Gg Hh Ii Jj
Kk Ll Mm Nn Oo
Pp Qq Rr Ss Tt Uu
Vv Ww Xx Yy Zz

60

Read My Lips

Let students practice elocution for the deaf in the tradition of Alexander Graham Bell, the inventor of the telephone. Bell, a teacher of the deaf, learned *elocution* (showing people how to speak correctly) from his father, who invented *Visible Speech*. Visible Speech was a code of symbols that illustrated positions of the mouth while speaking. Bell believed that by teaching deaf people to speak aloud, they would be less isolated. Let pairs of students tell each other simple phrases without making any sound, then guess what was said by taking turns studying the position of each others' mouths and lips.

Sign of the Times

Sign language, in all its forms, is the fourth most common language in the world. Have students practice this way of communicating. Explain that sign language is showing with your hands what you want to communicate. In the United States, American Sign Language (ASL) and Basic Sign Language (BSL) are used. ASL uses one hand, and BSL uses two. ASL is a mix of French Sign Language and *Ameraind* (used by American Indians for intertribal communication). Teach students a few words in ASL, then ask them to come up with their own signs for their names. Signs for names sometimes combine a characteristic of a person with a few letters in that person's name. Let students demonstrate their name signs, then tell how they came up with the signs and what they mean.

Helen Keller

Take a tip from Helen Keller: learning to speak is an enlightening experience! Let students practice communicating like Helen Keller, a blind and deaf woman born in 1880 who became a college graduate and famous lecturer. Taking advice from Alexander Graham Bell, Keller's parents hired a teacher for her named Anne Sullivan. Sullivan taught Helen to spell words by drawing letters in the palm of her hand. Helen also learned to communicate by using *Tadoma*: pressing her fingers against a speaker's lips to "hear" the words with her fingers. Have one student take a turn being Anne Sullivan by tracing letters on a partner's palm while her partner's eyes are closed. Can her partner guess what letters are being "written?" Let the partners trade roles and repeat the exercise with another word.

Making Music in-Our-Schools

Sound the trumpets and bang the drums! March is Music in Our Schools month! Whet students' appetites for musical knowledge with informative activities and homemade instruments.

Did You Know?

○ Ludwig van Beethoven was completely deaf when he wrote his *Ninth Symphony*.

○ Wolfgang Amadeus Mozart composed his first piece of music at age five.

○ A piano has 36 black and 52 white keys (88 total).

○ A typical symphony orchestra has over 100 instruments.

Literature Selections

The Nutcracker Suite by Peter Ilyich Tchaikovsky: Ambassador, 1994. (Compact Disc). Recording of the music from the popular ballet.

Peter and the Wolf by Sergei Prokofiev: Random House, 1994. (Book and audio cassette). The classic tale of Peter and the Wolf as told by Prokofiev's instrumental characters.

Pictures at an Exhibition by Modest Mussorgsky: Sony, 1972 (Compact Disc). Contains the title track and other works.

Zin Zin Zin! a Violin by Lloyd Moss: Aladdin Paperbacks, 2000. (Picture book, 32 pg.) An entertaining introduction to musical instruments and musical groups.

Learning to Read

Learning to read music is easy if you know the secret! Explain that a music staff is like handwriting lines used for writing notes instead of words. Give each student a copy of the music staff pattern (page 68) and help her label the notes. The notes are named for letters from A to G, and are listed from bottom to top on the staff. The notes in the spaces between the staff lines spell F-A-C-E , while the notes on the lines spell E-G-B-D-F. Use the mnemonic device *Every Good Boy Does Fine* to remember. These letters are repeated up and down the scale to create higher and lower tones. Combined with the time signature and indications for tempo and dynamics, music is simply different combinations of these notes! Let students look at actual sheet music to see if they recognize any notes.

Tempo and Dynamics

How do musicians know how quickly and loudly to play? *Tempo* is how fast or slow the beat is in a piece of music and *dynamics* is the loudness or softness of music. Begin by teaching tempo. On the board, write the words below.

Using their voices, feet, hands, or the instruments in the activities on pages 66-67, call out a tempo and let students play it. Next, work on dynamics. On the board, write and draw symbols for the words below.

Tempo:
largo = *very slow*
andante = *walking pace*
allegro = *lively*
presto = *very fast*

Dynamics:
piano = *soft* = *p*
forte – *loud* = *f*
crescendo = *gradually get louder* = <
decrescendo = *gradually get softer* = >

Music and Dance

All this music will make students want to dance! Explain that listening for rhythm and understanding tempo and dynamics helps when deciding how to move to a piece of music. Talk about dance rhythms (samba, waltz, march, etc.). Ask students why these dances are different (they have different tempos, different rhythms, etc.). Then, let students experiment. Play excerpts from the *Nutcracker Suite* by Tchaikovsky while students dance. Between each piece, have students describe the tempo and dynamics, then tell students the name of the piece and ask why students think it was given its particular name (*Dance of the Sugarplum Fairy, Waltz of the Flowers,* etc.). When several excerpts have been played, talk about what kinds of movements match each tempo and dynamic.

Pass the Rhythm

Feel the rhythm of your name! *Rhythm* is a pattern of long and short notes. Have students sit in a circle. Say your name as you clap along to its rhythm, then clap the same rhythm without speaking. Let students clap the rhythm of your name. Have a student clap the rhythm of his name, then have the class clap along. Continue until each student has clapped her name. If desired, display copies of the note patterns (page 68). Explain that in common time in music, a whole note is equal to four beats, a half note is equal to two beats, a quarter note is equal to one beat, and an eighth note is equal to half a beat. Hold up each note and ask students to clap the number of beats for each note.

Name that Music!

Strike up a study of several types of music. Each week, feature a different genre of music, such as classical, jazz, rock-and-roll, country, folk, etc. Play music from that genre each morning. Write each genre on a large, colorful sentence strip and display on a bulletin board. Have students research composers and musicians, instruments, etc., from the featured genre and write facts and favorite songs on index cards accented with note patterns (page 68). Display the notes under the correct headings on the bulletin board. At the end of the week, ask students to write short paragraphs characterizing the featured genre and display them on the bulletin board.

Can You See What I Hear?

Let students "see" music as they listen to it. *Programmed music* was written by composers to send the listener on a journey through their minds as the work unfolds. Modest Petrovich Mussorgsky's *Pictures at an Exhibition* is a great example. As the music plays, the listener is to visualize a stout man walking through a museum stopping to look at paintings. Each painting has its own tune and gives the listener the feeling that he is looking at it! Give each student several pieces of paper. Play excerpts from this piece, such as *The Gnome, The Old Castle, Ballet of the Chicks in their Shells*, etc., without telling students the name of the excerpt. Have each student draw a picture for each excerpt based on what he visualizes during the music. When all the pictures are complete, tell students the titles. Are there similarities between their drawings and the titles? Display the pictures on a bulletin board titled *The Pictures at Our Exhibition*.

The Pictures at Our Exhibition

Tell Me a Story

Now that students can see the music, it is time for them to *be* the music! First, talk about how stories are set to music in operas, musicals, ballets, etc. Read the story of *Peter and the Wolf* to the class. Play the music from *Peter and the Wolf* and explain that each instrument represents a different character in the story. After listening, talk about why each instrument was appropriate for its character, then divide students into small groups. Have each group write a story. Each character in the story must have a different sound or instrument to represent him. Students may wish to use their musical instruments made in class, (pages 66-67) or simply whistle, clap, etc. When the stories are complete, have each group perform its story for the class.

Round and Round We Go!

Create a circle of music! Explain that a *round* is sung when two or more groups of singers sing a song, starting at the beginning of the song but at different times. Pick a simple song, such as *Row, Row, Row Your Boat* or *London Bridge*. Divide the class into two groups. Have the first group start the song, then have the second group join in after the first group has completed the first line. Keep dividing students into smaller and smaller groups and listen to how the melody, sung together at different intervals, creates harmony.

Example:
Group 1: Row, row, row your boat

Group 1: Gently down the stream
Group 2: Row, row, row your boat

Group 1: Merrily, merrily, merrily, merrily
Group 2: Gently down the stream

Group 1: Life is but a dream
Group 2: Merrily, merrily, merrily, merrily

Group 2: Life is but a dream

We've Got Spirit!

Show school spirit and classroom pride with a class song. Explain that words to a song are called *lyrics* and the tune is called the *melody*. Brainstorm a list of words to describe class attitude, curriculum, people, etc. Then, choose a familiar song, such as *Twinkle, Twinkle Little Star*, and write it on an overhead projector, leaving space between the lines. Write the new lyrics for the song, using the same melody, above the old words to work out the rhythm and rhyme. Sing the class song on field trips, during class activities, open house, etc., to foster class spirit and a team environment.

Mrs. Johnson's Class Song
(Sing to the tune of *Twinkle, Twinkle Little Star*)
We are Mrs. Johnson's crew.
We work hard at all we do.
Math and reading, science too,
If it's old or if it's new.
We are Mrs. Johnson's crew.
We work hard at all we do.

Thanks for the Music

Note how great the school music teacher is with a big thank you! Enlarge an eighth note pattern (page 68) for each student and have her write a thank-you note on it with white pencil or crayon. When all of the thank-yous are complete, tape them to a long piece of string. Hang the thank-you banner in the music teacher's classroom.

65

Music Anytime

Play what you have! Read the poem "Ourchestra" from *Where the Sidewalk Ends* by Shel Silverstein (HarperCollins Juvenile Books, 1974) to the class. Tell each student to think of a unique way to make sound using only hands, fingers, mouth, etc. Then, let students make music! Have each child think of a name for his instrument or musical technique and present it to the class. Then, let the class play to the tune of a familiar song.

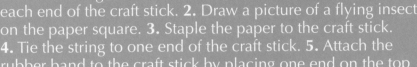

Nature's Music

A stream running, a bug flying, frogs croaking—all of these are nature's music! Mimic the sound of flying bugs with hummers. Give each student a craft stick, two rectangular pencil erasers, a large rubber band, a 3" x 3" square of paper, and 3' of string. **1.** Place an eraser on each end of the craft stick. **2.** Draw a picture of a flying insect on the paper square. **3.** Staple the paper to the craft stick. **4.** Tie the string to one end of the craft stick. **5.** Attach the rubber band to the craft stick by placing one end on the top of each eraser. **6.** Then, take students to an open area and spin the hummers in circles. How does the sound change as the hummer is spun more quickly?

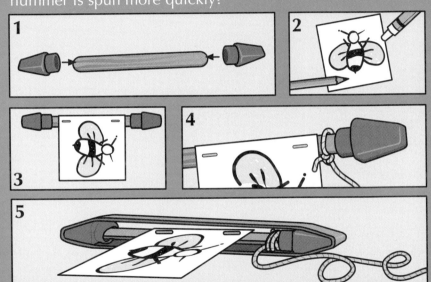

Feel the Vibrations!

Ride the wave of sound vibration with kazoos! Sound is created by vibrations called *sound waves* moving through the air. When the waves reach our eardrums, they send messages to our brains which we interpret as sound. To demonstrate this concept, have students place their hands on their throats, then say "We love music!" Ask if they can feel their vocal cords vibrating. Next, give each student a short cardboard tube, a piece of waxed paper, and a rubber band. Punch a hole about 1/4" from the end of one side of the tube. Wrap the waxed paper over the same end, leaving the punched hole exposed, and secure it with a rubber band. Have each student hum loudly into the open end of the tube, while placing her fingers lightly on the waxed paper at the other end. Have students describe what the vibrations feel and sound like, then ask a volunteer to play a tune!

Pitch-Perfect Pan Pipes

Some instruments need the wind to work! Wind instruments must have air blown through them to produce sound. They produce high or low pitches depending on the length of each instrument's air passage. The longer the air passage, the lower the pitch. Different methods are used to change the length of the passage. The slide is moved on a trombone, holes are covered and uncovered on a clarinet and flute, etc. Demonstrate how wind instruments work with pan flutes. Have each student cut five straws into five different lengths. Then, let students decorate one side of a cardboard triangle, then place the straws in order from shortest to longest on the plain side, and tape them down. Finally, let students blow into each straw and listen to the pitches, and even make up their own songs on their pan pipes!

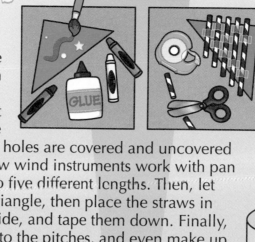

Musical Buttons

Everyone's heard of musical chairs, but what about musical buttons? Make simple percussion instruments from socks and buttons. *Percussion* means "the act of striking." Brainstorm a list of percussion instruments with students, (drums, xylophones, bells, etc.). Give each student a large sock and several large, plastic buttons. Let each student decorate her sock and glue or sew the buttons to one side, then put the sock over her hand, puppet-style. Play the instruments by tapping them on a hard surface or by touching fingers to thumbs. Form a percussion band by letting some students play their button socks, while others tap pencils on desks, rub sandpaper together, clap hands, etc.

Stringing Along

Ready for something ex"string"ly fun? Make stringed instruments! Explain that stringed instruments produce sound vibrations by being plucked or bowed. Name several stringed instruments (violin, guitar, harp, etc.), then give each student a large rubber band. Provide different sized cups, boxes, plastic containers, etc. Let each student choose a large and a small container. Have students wrap a rubber band around each container so the bands stretch over the openings, and pluck them. Is the pitch high or low? Then, have students pluck the rubber bands over their other containers and listen for the pitch again. Which containers produce high pitches and which produce low pitches? (The tighter the rubber band is stretched, the higher the pitch it will produce when plucked.) Explain that this principle is used in tuning stringed instruments.

67

© Carson-Dellosa CD-2096

half note

quarter note

eighth note

whole note

music staff

treble clef
(use with bulletin board idea pg. 17)

COPY and CUT

68

© Carson-Dellosa CD-2096

St. Patrick's Day

St. Patrick's Day is celebrated in honor of Saint Patrick, the patron saint of Ireland, who died on March 17, around 460 A.D. Saint Patrick was actually born in Wales, but he moved to Ireland to teach the people about Christianity. In Ireland, St. Patrick's Day is primarily a religious occasion. Schools and offices are closed. Many families attend mass and community gatherings. Some people wear shamrocks, a symbol of good luck. In other countries, the celebration is usually nonreligious. Many people wear green clothing and attend parties and parades.

Did You Know?

🍀 Green is the color of Saint Patrick's Day because it is the color of spring, Ireland, and the shamrock.
🍀 According to legend, Saint Patrick drove all the snakes out of Ireland by beating a drum.
🍀 According to Irish folklore, a leprechaun is an elf that hides from humans and other leprechauns.
🍀 The first American St. Patrick's Day celebration took place in Boston, Massachusetts in 1737.

Literature Selections

Leprechaun Gold by Teresa Bateman: Holiday House, Inc., 1998. (Picture book, 32 pg.) Donald O'Dell refuses a leprechaun's gold but is still rewarded in an unexpected fashion.
Lucky O'Leprechaun by Jana Dillon: Pelican Publishing Co. (Picture book, 32 pg.) Two children catch a leprechaun and get to make a wish.
The Story of St. Patrick by James A. Janda: Paulist Press, 1995. (Picture book, 32 pg.) A detailed biography of Saint Patrick.

Glittering Green and Gold Flags

Irish eyes will be smiling at this St. Patrick's Day flag. The Irish flag was originally green with a gold harp in the center. It is now green, white, and orange. Some people call the orange "gold" in reference to the gold harp on the old flag. Let students put the green and gold on an Irish flag. Provide a large piece of white poster board divided into three equal, vertical sections. Copy shamrock patterns (page 76) on green paper and gold coin patterns (page 76) on orange paper. Give one of each pattern to each student. Let students decorate the patterns with glitter. Have students glue shamrock patterns in the left section of the flag and gold coin patterns in the right section. Leave the middle section white. Display the flag during your St. Patrick's Day unit.

69

A Bonny Banner

Spread the word that it's St. Patrick's Day with a classroom banner. Let students decorate a large piece of white butcher paper using shamrock patterns (page 76), pot of gold patterns (page 78), and art supplies. Provide green pepper halves and green paint for students to print shamrock shapes, and small potato halves and gold paint to print gold coin shapes. Write an Irish saying across the banner, such as *Erin Go Bragh,* which means *Ireland Forever.* Display the banner on a wall outside the classroom.

Dance an Irish Jig

Jump up and down for St. Patrick's Day with an Irish jig. Step dances were created by Irish dancing masters who traveled from town to town improvising steps to fit the local music. In the traditional Irish Jig, dancers keep their hands at their sides and move their feet in springy steps. Celebrate St. Patrick's Day by teaching children an Irish Jig.

Stand with feet together and hands at sides.
Put your left foot forward and to the side.
Tap the heel of your left foot while you hop once on your right foot.
Hop again on your right foot, then bring your left foot to the front and tap your toe.
Hop on your right foot again and bring the left foot to the side.
Hop on your right foot again and put both feet back together with a stomp. Repeat, using alternating feet.
After students have practiced the steps, play Irish music and let them show off their skills.

Irish Soda Bread

Give students a taste of Ireland with Irish soda bread, a common accompaniment to Irish meals.
3 1/2 cups flour
1 teaspoon sugar
1 teaspoon salt
1 teaspoon baking soda
1 cup plus a few tablespoons of buttermilk
Preheat oven to 450°. Sift dry ingredients several times. Make a well in the center and pour in three-fourths of the buttermilk and stir. Slowly add the rest of the buttermilk. Place the dough on a flour-covered surface and knead for 30 seconds. Flatten the dough and place on a floured baking sheet. Use a sharp knife to cut a deep cross in the top half of the dough. Bake for 45 minutes. Serve each student a slice of the bread with a wee bit o' green (cream cheese or butter mixed with green food coloring).

Whimsical Walking Sticks

A *shillelagh* (shi•LAY•lee), which literally means oak club in Irish, is an Irish walking stick. Make a special class shillelagh for St. Patrick's Day. Provide a wrapping paper tube and have students decorate it with Irish symbols, such as pots of gold, shamrocks, and leprechauns. Crumple green paper into a ball and tape it to the top of the tube. On St. Patrick's Day, let line leaders carry the shillelagh or have students use it as a special hall pass.

Look All Over for a Four-Leaf Clover

Find out who has the real luck o' the Irish! Finding a four-leaf clover or shamrock on St. Patrick's Day means twice the good luck. Copy several shamrock patterns (page 76) and two or three four-leaf clover patterns (page 77). Hide the patterns around the room before students arrive at school. Then, have students search the room for the shamrocks and clovers. Let students who find the four-leaf clovers use them as free homework passes. No homework? Now, that's lucky!

Good Luck Charms

Luck will follow students when they make these charms. Enlarge a shamrock pattern on tagboard for each child. Have each student decorate her shamrock with green items cut from magazines. Students should fill their shamrocks completely. Next, punch holes around the outside of the pattern and let students use gold ribbon to lace through the holes. Tie the ribbon and let students take the good luck charms home to share.

Bit o' Green Books

I spy a bit o' green! Let students look around the classroom for green objects, but make sure they do not tell what they see. Pass out a sheet of paper to each student. Have each student write several clues to her favorite green object, beginning her clues with *I spy a bit o' green*. Clues might include *I spy a bit o' green by the clock* or *I spy a bit o' green on the teacher's desk*. Then, on the back of the paper, have each student draw her green object and label it. Bind the pages in a class book called *A Bit o' Green in Mrs. _____'s Class*. Have students look through the book and try to guess the objects before turning the pages to see the answers.

71

Kissing the Blarney Stone

The *Blarney Stone* is a stone in the wall of Ireland's Blarney Castle. Kissing the stone is said to bring good luck to the kisser. Legend has it that an old woman cast a spell on the stone to reward a king who saved her from drowning. Kissing the stone gave the king the "gift of gab" (ability to speak convincingly). Let students imagine what kind of magic stone they would like to have. Take students outside to find rocks. Wash the rocks and let students decorate them with paint, glitter, sequins, etc. Let students make up legends about their decorated stones, including how they became lucky or magical and what they will do for their owners.

Emerald Isle Poems

Green reminds people of the many green pastures and fields that cover the Emerald Isle. Find out what the color green brings to students' minds with this sensory poem. Ask students "How does the color green taste? How does it smell?" Give each child an enlarged copy of the shamrock pattern (page 76). Instruct him to write sentences about how green looks, tastes, smells, sounds, and feels. Let students decorate the shamrocks and share their poems with the class. Write your own poem on a four-leaf clover pattern (page 77). Draw a large outline of Ireland on butcher paper, cut it out, and staple it to a bulletin board. Display the green poems together covering the island and let students find your poem among theirs.

Example Poem:
Green looks like the sea.
Green tastes like sweet candy.
Green smells like watermelon slices on a hot summer day.
Green sounds like waves crashing on the beach.
Green feels like a soft field of clover.

Golden Harps

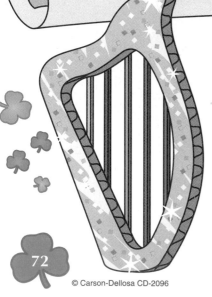

The harp is heard in many traditional Irish songs. Before televisions and radios, people gathered to hear poets play the harp and recite verse. Many people were sent to Ireland to learn to play the harp. Let students make Irish harp music. Give each child a large square of cardboard, trace the harp pattern (page 77) on the cardboard, and cut it out, including the center portion. Have each student turn over his harp and staple rubber bands across the back to resemble strings. Provide glitter, crayons, etc., and let students decorate their harps. Then, explain that the Irish harp is held on the knee and strummed. If possible, play traditional Irish music and let students "play along" with their harps.

72

If I Caught a Leprechaun...

Irish legend describes leprechauns as shoemaker elves who will lead you to their hidden gold if you catch them. What would you do if you caught a leprechaun? Let students answer with this craft and story activity. Give each student a leprechaun pattern (page 77) to color, and a resealable plastic bag. Have students "catch" their leprechauns in their bags after coloring. On a sheet of paper, let each student write what she would do if she caught a leprechaun. Staple the bags to the stories and let students read them during free time.

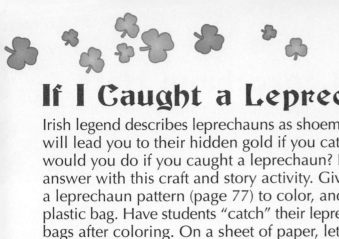

Leprechaun Hat Treat Cups

Hats off to these leprechaun treats! Give each student a small paper plate and cup. Trace the mouth of the cup in the center of the paper plate and cut out the circle. Next, have students paint their plates and cups green, and, if desired, decorate them with glitter and sequins. Let each student cut out a square of construction paper, decorate it to look like a hat buckle, then glue it to the cup. Finally, insert the cup bottom into the paper plate hole and slide it down to fit, creating a hat. Let students leave their leprechaun hats on windowsills to dry. Before students arrive at school the next day, put candy treats wrapped in gold foil in each hat. Let students find their hats and enjoy their treats. You may wish to use this activity in place of the treat bags in *A Leprechaun Was Here* (page 74).

Searching for a Pot of Gold

Let students help Lucky Leprechaun find his missing gold. Pass out the Leprechaun Maze worksheet (page 75) for each student to solve. As students solve the puzzle, reward them with a small piece of green or gold candy, such as chocolate coins wrapped in gold foil.

73

Dandy Leprechaun Hats

Turn students into leprechauns with these festive hats. For each student, cut a 2" wide strip of paper long enough to fit around her head with approximately 1" left at each end. Give each student a copy of the leprechaun hat pattern (page 76) to decorate. Then, have each student glue her hat pattern to a paper strip. Glue or tape the ends together to form a headband. Provide green finger paint and let each student make a thumbprint shamrock to cut out and glue to the side of her hat. Let students wear their leprechaun hats while participating in *Dance an Irish Jig* (page 70).

A Leprechaun Was Here!

Catch a leprechaun! Let students make leprechaun traps from shoeboxes. Have students turn over the boxes and decorate them in a way they think would appeal to leprechauns. Let students prop up the traps with pencils. Before students arrive in the morning, cut tiny leprechaun footprints from green construction paper, and move a few things around to make the room look as if a leprechaun visited. Spring a few traps and place small items inside, such as clovers or chocolate candies wrapped in gold foil. Place a treat bag for each student on the windowsill. When students arrive, tell them a leprechaun visited the night before. Check the traps to see if students have caught him, then enjoy the treats he left behind.

My hiding place would be under my dog's house in the back yard. I have a big German Shepherd dog and she will bark at anyone who looks under her doghouse.

Chris

Where Would You Hide the Gold?

Those wee leprechauns usually hide their pots of gold at the ends of rainbows. What would be a more secret place? Let students pretend to be leprechauns with a very important job—finding a safe place to hide gold! Give each student an enlarged pot of gold pattern (page 78) and have him write where his hiding place would be and why. When the stories are complete, let students share them with the class. Display the stories on a bulletin board or wall at the end of a rainbow.

74

Name _____

Leprechaun Maze

Help Lucky Leprechaun find his pot of gold!

leprechaun hat

COPY and CUT

shamrock

gold coin
(also use with bulletin board pattern, page 18)

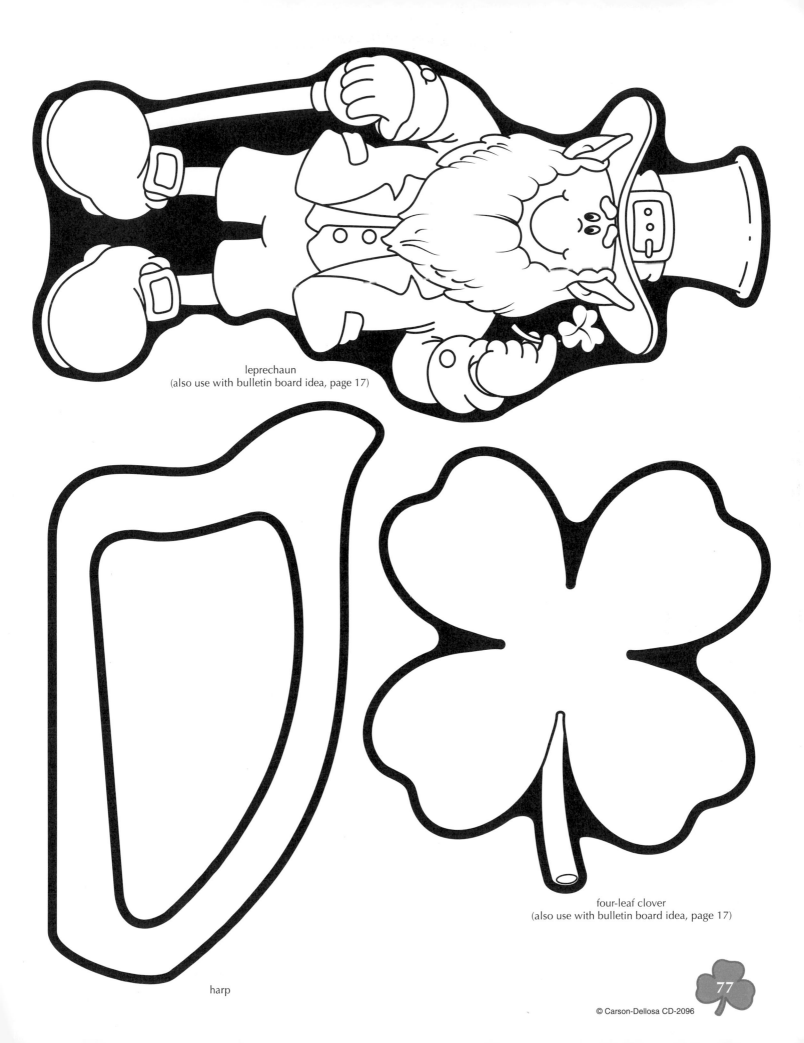

leprechaun
(also use with bulletin board idea, page 17)

four-leaf clover
(also use with bulletin board idea, page 17)

harp

77

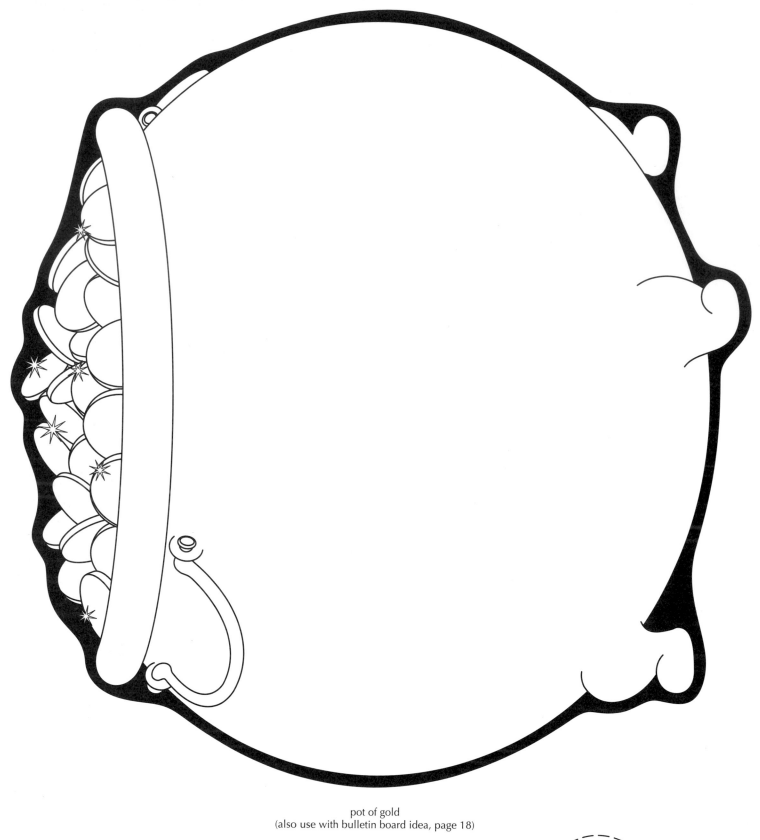

pot of gold
(also use with bulletin board idea, page 18)

COPY and CUT

78

Rainbows and Colors

Even if there is no pot of gold at the end, students will be delighted to explore all the colors of the rainbow!

Did You Know?

- Every rainbow is a full circle. The full circle cannot be seen from the ground but may be observed from an airplane.
- In England, students remember the colors of the rainbow (red, orange, yellow, green, blue, indigo, violet) with a history lesson—Richard of York Gave Battle In Vain.
- The human eye can see 7 million colors.
- Scientists have discovered that the appropriate use of color can maximize productivity, minimize visual fatigue, and relax the body. Red, orange, and yellow are thought to be stimulating; while pale green, light yellow, and off-white are thought to be soothing.

Literature Selections

A Rainbow of My Own by Don Freeman: Viking Press, 1978. A small boy imagines what it would be like to have his own rainbow to play with.

Swinging on a Rainbow by Charles Perkins: Africa World Press, Inc., 1993. (Storybook, 32 pg.) Patrice fulfills her dream of swinging on a rainbow and finds that it is not far away, but right in her back yard.

Hailstones and Halibut Bones by Mary O'Neil: Doubleday, 1989 (Poetry collection, 61 pg.) An illustrated version of O'Neil's classic book of poetry exploring the colors of the spectrum.

Make a Rainbow

Create a rainbow for students to see! Go outside on a sunny day and position students with the sun behind them and slightly to the side. Spray water from a bottle and a rainbow should appear in the spray. Explain that the sunlight is made of all the different colors of light, which appear white when combined. When sunlight hits water, the light waves move more slowly through water than they do through light. Because some wavelengths are longer than others, they break away from each other, and we see the rainbow. The same thing happens when we see rainbows in the sky. Each raindrop acts as a tiny *prism* (see *The Magic of Prisms*, page 80), by breaking sunlight into its seven colors. Introduce students to Roy G. Biv to help them remember the colors of the rainbow in order—red, orange, yellow, green, blue, indigo, violet.

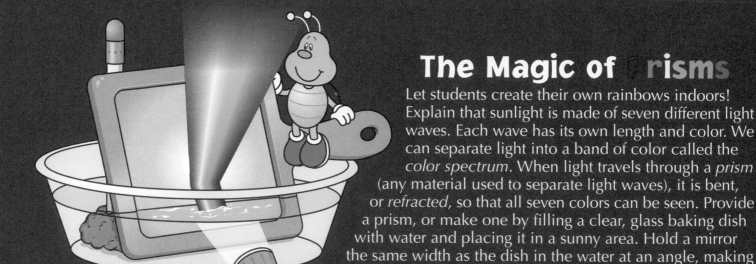

The Magic of Prisms

Let students create their own rainbows indoors! Explain that sunlight is made of seven different light waves. Each wave has its own length and color. We can separate light into a band of color called the *color spectrum*. When light travels through a *prism* (any material used to separate light waves), it is bent, or *refracted*, so that all seven colors can be seen. Provide a prism, or make one by filling a clear, glass baking dish with water and placing it in a sunny area. Hold a mirror the same width as the dish in the water at an angle, making a triangular wedge of water. When the water surface is settled, gently move the mirror back and forth until you see a rainbow on the wall. If you do not have enough sunlight, shine a flashlight on the portion of the mirror that is under water. When you see the rainbow, work with the prism until you get the brightest, widest possible spectrum, then prop up a pencil in modeling clay, and lean the mirror gently against it. Make sure the surface behind the rainbow is white (attach white poster board to the wall if necessary). Have students observe carefully and draw pictures of the spectrum they see, choosing crayon colors as accurately as possible.

Reflecting and Absorbing Colors

After separating light with a prism, put it back together! Cover three flashlights with red, green, and blue plastic wrap (the primary colors of light). Darken the room and let students shine the lights on a wall to show the separate colors. Then, overlap the beams and the light will appear white! To further demonstrate how combinations of light work, put a red, blue, and green ball on a desk. (Use inflated balloons if balls are not available.) Shine the flashlight with the red lens on the balls. Only the red ball will look red; the other two will look black. Repeat using the other lenses. Explain to students that objects reflect and absorb different colors of light. We say a red ball is red, but actually it is every other color except red. This is because the ball absorbs all colors of light waves except red. It reflects the red light waves, so we see red. Black objects absorb all colors of light and do not reflect any light. White objects reflect all of the colors in the spectrum, which when mixed produce white. This explains why black shirts are so much hotter than white shirts: they do not allow any of the light waves to escape, and they absorb all of the heat as well!

Rainbow Spinners

Rainbow spinners show once again that all the colors of light make...white! Give each child a copy of the rainbow spinner (page 84) on white card stock to cut out. Instruct her to use crayons to color each section a different spectral color. Poke a pencil point through the two dots on the pattern. Thread a long piece of heavy string through the holes, then tie the ends together. Hold each end of the loop. Twist the circle around several times so that the string "winds up," then, pull the ends of the string to spin the circle. When the circle spins slowly, all the colors appear. When the circle spins quickly, students will see a mixture of all seven colors, which will appear white.

zizzzzz...

Stained Glass Rainbows

Display a rainbow of colors with symmetrical sun catchers. Tape a 17" length of plastic wrap to a work surface for each student. Have students cut or tear colorful tissue paper into small pieces and glue them to the plastic wrap in rainbow order. Give each child a piece of black construction paper slightly larger than the plastic wrap. Fold it in half horizontally, then vertically, and cut shapes into the paper along both edges where there is a fold. Open up the black paper and notice the symmetrical design created. Glue the black paper over the tissue paper design. When dry, display on a window to let the sun shine through.

Color Mixing

Let students observe color mixing and then mix colors on palettes—just like professional painters! Fill several small, clear cups with water and place them on an overhead projector. Add a few drops of red food coloring to one cup of water, add yellow to another, and blue to a third. Mix the primary colors in other cups to make secondary colors. Quiz students on the primary colors (red, yellow, and blue) and which combinations form secondary colors (blue + yellow = green, yellow + red = orange, and red + blue = purple). Then, give each child a copy of the artist's palette (page 84) on heavy card stock. Explain that a palette is used by artists as a surface on which to mix colors. Have students add water colors to the appropriate primary areas (see illustration) and use those colors to create the secondary colors.

81

Kaleidoscope Colors

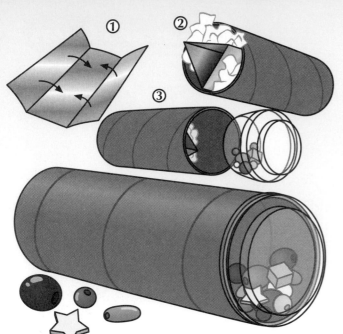

Make a kaleidoscope full of colorful surprises! Copy the kaleidoscope insert pattern (page 84) on mylar-coated construction paper, or cut sections from a mylar balloon and use rubber cement to glue them to poster board which has been cut from the pattern. Fold along the dotted lines (with the mylar surface on the inside) to form a triangular insert. Let students place the shape into a short cardboard tube and wedge crumpled paper between the tube and the insert to hold it in place. Place colorful glass beads, sequins, or buttons in a small, clear cup that will fit into one end of the tube. Cap the cup with a clear lid. Rotate the cap of the container to view the colorful display.

Dip-and-Dye Paper Towels

Dye paper towels to make attractive color journal covers. Add red, yellow, and blue food coloring to small bowls of water to make concentrated solutions. Give each student a white paper towel to fold into a small square. Have students dip the corners of their squares in the different bowls. As the paper towels absorb the water, the colors blend to produce secondary colors. Carefully unfold the paper towels to see the patterns, then dry them overnight. Then, use rubber cement to glue the paper towels to cardboard cut to the desired cover size. Fold the edges of the paper towel over the cardboard and glue. You may wish to insert a page for each color your class is studying, then have students record their feelings, observations, etc., about each color.

Camouflaged Crayons

How do you hide a crayon? Challenge students to answer this question as you make a class color book called *How to Hide a Crayon*. Give each student a different colored crayon and have him think of an object that is that color. For example, a yellow crayon can hide in a pitcher of lemonade, a black crayon can hide in the night sky, etc. Have each student create a picture containing her particular color. Then, glue the crayon to the picture to "hide" the crayon. Use large binder rings to bind the pages into a class book titled *How to Hide a Crayon* and place at a reading center.

82

Pointillism Pictures

Get to the point of secondary colors with *pointillism*, a painting technique in which the artist uses tiny dots of paint to create the illusion that colors blend. Show artwork by pointillist Georges Seurat. Then, instruct students to draw primary-colored pictures that will appear to contain secondary colors (green, orange, purple). Have students make light pencil drawings, and then dip cotton swabs into watercolor paint and fill in the color. Place primary color dots (red, yellow, blue) close to each other to form secondary colors. For example, dots of red and yellow placed close together will appear orange at a distance. Post the pointillism pictures on a far wall of the classroom and let students observe the new colors!

Rainbow Salad

Create a rainbow salad for snack time. Let students help layer the fruits listed below in clear, plastic cups in the order of Roy G. Biv. Top with a whipped cream cloud!

Red	Strawberry slices
Orange	Orange slices
Yellow	Pineapple chunks or Banana slices
Green	Sliced Kiwi or Green Grapes
Blue	Blueberries
Indigo and Violet	Purple Grapes

Colorful Cupcakes

Allow students to experiment with color mixing at snack time! Give each student a cupcake that is frosted with whipped topping or white frosting. On the whipped topping, place one drop of red, one drop of blue, and one drop of yellow food coloring (each of the primary colors) spacing them equally apart. Give each student a craft stick to mix the primary colors. Instruct student to mix the yellow and blue to make green, the red and yellow to make orange, and the red and blue to make purple.

83

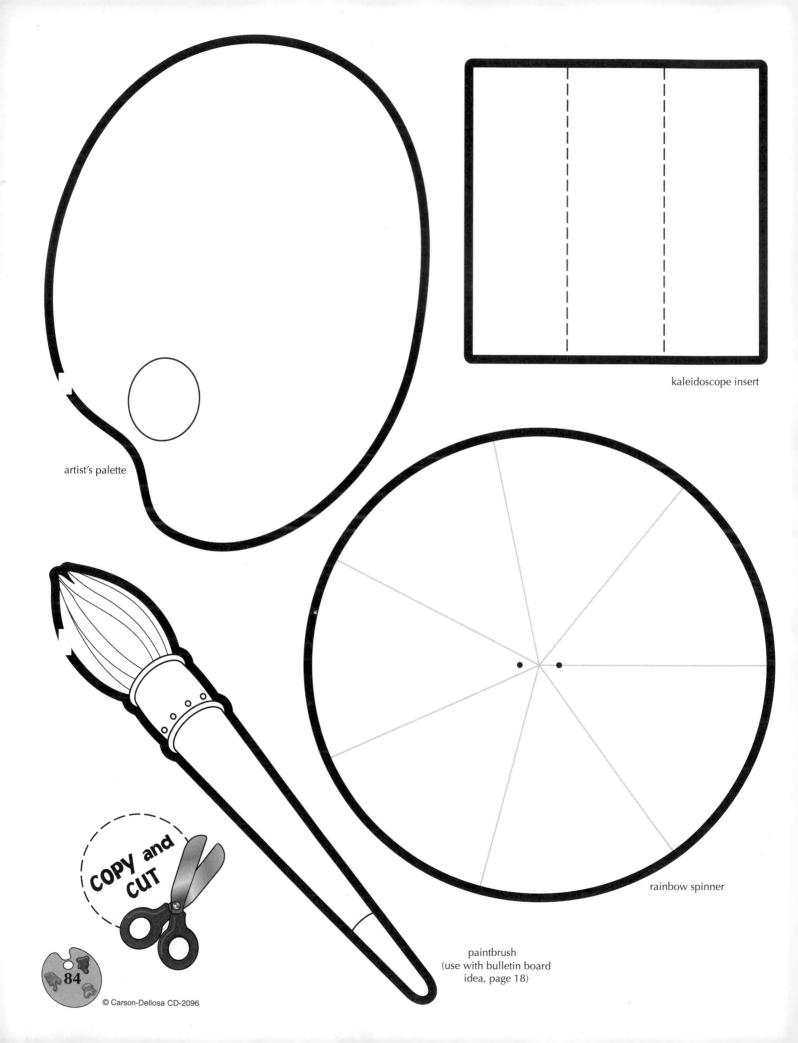

artist's palette

kaleidoscope insert

rainbow spinner

COPY and CUT

paintbrush
(use with bulletin board
idea, page 18)

84

© Carson-Dellosa CD-2096

Food For Thought

If you are what you eat, is it better to be one smart cookie or a couch potato? Teach students about National Nutrition Month® in March.

Did You Know?

- President Thomas Jefferson served french fries to guests at a White House dinner in 1802.
- Pizza originated in Italy in the early 16th century. Noodles came from China, much earlier.
- Recommended servings for children are: milk group: 2-4 servings, meat group: 2 servings, vegetable group: 3 servings, fruit group: 2 servings, bread group: 6 servings, fats and sweets: use sparingly.
- The best way to get complete nutrition is to eat a wide variety of foods.

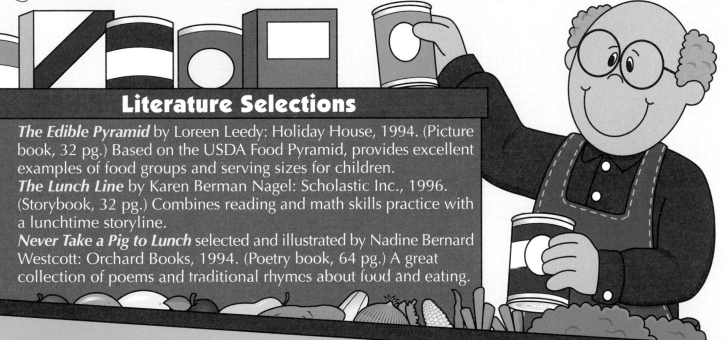

Literature Selections

The Edible Pyramid by Loreen Leedy: Holiday House, 1994. (Picture book, 32 pg.) Based on the USDA Food Pyramid, provides excellent examples of food groups and serving sizes for children.

The Lunch Line by Karen Berman Nagel: Scholastic Inc., 1996. (Storybook, 32 pg.) Combines reading and math skills practice with a lunchtime storyline.

Never Take a Pig to Lunch selected and illustrated by Nadine Bernard Westcott: Orchard Books, 1994. (Poetry book, 64 pg.) A great collection of poems and traditional rhymes about food and eating.

3-Dimensional Food Pyramid

Help students grasp the dimensions of the food pyramid. Give each student a copy of the blank food pyramid pattern (page 92) to cut out, and a sheet of 8½" x 11" paper. **1.** Fold the paper in half horizontally and place the pattern along the fold. **2.** Trace the pattern onto the folded paper. Cut along the traced edges, leaving the folded edge intact. **3.** The resulting diamond shape will form the two remaining pyramid sides. **4.** Tape the diamond shape to the pyramid pattern on one side. Orient the papers as shown. On one side of the diamond, have students draw pictures of themselves eating healthy foods. On the other side, have them write healthy menu plans. On the blank pyramid pattern, have children write the food items from their menu plans in the correct sections. **5.** Tape the remaining sides together.

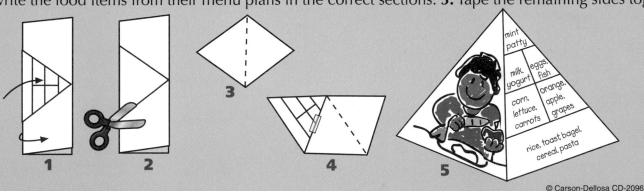

Food Group Projects

The food pyramid is more than meat, milk, and bread! Highlight the many options in each food group by having students present food group projects while hosting Healthy Snack Week. Divide students into six groups and assign each a day of the week and a food category to study and present as a poster, mobile, oral report, skit, etc. Ask groups to explore some of the more unusual foods in each group. For a five-day schedule, allow two groups to present on one day. On each day, have the assigned group bring healthy snacks from that category for students to enjoy after the presentation. Save dessert (fats and sweets) for last, and if desired, let this group research and present healthy dessert alternatives!

Tracking Snacking

Make snack time productive by talking about its nutritional value. During snack time, list favorite snacks. Write and illustrate the snacks in columns according to the food group to which they belong. Make a column of vegetable snacks, sweet snacks, etc. Do not label the columns. Accordion-fold the chart and see if children can guess which food group each snack column represents. Discuss the tips below for healthy snacking habits, then ask students to think of alternative snacks. If desired, provide the alternative snacks for future snack times.
• Discourage "grazing." Only allow snacking at predetermined times and places.
• If children participate in choosing snacks, they will be more likely to eat them.
• Avoid sugary, artificial juices and caffeinated beverages.
• Remember that snacks do not have to be sweet, sticky, or gooey—only delicious!

Food Pyramid Bean Bag Toss

Target healthy meals with a group game. Draw and label a large food pyramid on poster board. Label the pyramid sections. Explain that small groups will take turns tossing bean bags onto the pyramid, rotating turns within groups. The object is to be the first group to complete a healthy day by scoring a predetermined number of "servings" from each food group. See *Did You Know?* (page 85) for the recommended number of servings for children. To score a serving, students must toss the bean bag onto a section of the pyramid, name that food group, and name a food from that group. Students who miss the pyramid or land on a "full" food group lose their turn.

Food Pyramid Puzzle

Help students piece together an understanding of food groups. Using the food pyramid pattern (page 92) as a model, draw a large, blank food pyramid on butcher paper. Divide the class into six groups, cut apart the six pyramid sections, and have each group draw foods from its food group on the pyramid. Cut the illustrated sections into puzzle pieces and laminate. Mix up the pieces and let students reassemble the puzzles. If desired, let each group take a turn reassembling the entire pyramid.

Dietary Diary

Encourage responsible eating by having students keep food "diaries." After lunch, post a large copy of the food pyramid pattern (page 92) in the classroom. Provide each student with a blank food pyramid pattern (page 92) on which to list the foods he ate for breakfast and lunch, writing the foods and number of servings in the appropriate sections of the pyramid. Let students compare the lists with the recommended number of daily servings from each group (see *Did You Know?*, page 85), and plan a dinner to meet their needs for a healthy diet. If desired, staple several copies of the blank food pyramid pattern together for each child, and let him track his eating habits for a few days.

Food Category Relay Race

Fast food takes on new meaning with this grouping game! Assign students to four teams, each with its own blank food pyramid drawn on poster board. Let students cut pictures of foods from magazines and newspapers, until there are enough pictures to fill four food pyramids. Place the pictures in a box. Place the posters and the pictures on one side of the room. Line up each group across from a pyramid. Students should race to the box, choose a food picture, tape the picture to the correct category on their pyramid, and return to the end of the line so the next player can repeat the process. Students lose a turn if they choose a food from a "full" category. The winning group is the first to correctly tape a predetermined number of "servings" on its pyramid.

Junk Food Pyramid

After students plan a healthy daily diet, let them have fun planning a junk food menu. Give students copies of the blank food pyramid pattern (page 92) and let them plan a junk food diet. For example, a student could list *candy apple* for the fruit group, *peanut brittle* for protein, *carrot cake* for the vegetable group, etc. Challenge students to fill the entire pyramid. Afterward, have students consider the negative effects of a junk food diet and list more nutritious, equally enjoyable alternatives.

87

The Keys to Good Health

Improve students' knowledge about essential nutrients! Nutrients are important substances in food that provide energy, strength, and protection to the body. Nutrients help fight disease and keep the body growing and running smoothly. The six categories of nutrients are: *vitamins, minerals, proteins, carbohydrates, fats,* and *water.* Assign six nutrient groups. Have students go to the library or talk to health professionals to find out what each nutrient does for the body and what foods contain that nutrient. Students can present their findings to the class through reports, collages, mobiles, or posters. If desired, create a graph on the board with the headings *Nutrient, What it Does,* and *Where You Find It,* and have students fill in the information as it is discovered.

Nutrient	What it Does	Where You Find It
Vitamin A	repairs tissue, maintains eyesight	dark green, orange, yellow fruits and vegetables
Vitamin B group	releases nutrients, forms blood cells	vegetables, grains, fruits, some meats
Vitamin C	heals wounds, helps prevent infections	fruits and vegetables
Vitamin D	promotes calcium/phosphorus absorption	dairy products
calcium	maintains strong bones and teeth	dairy products
carbohydrates	supply energy	grains, vegetables, fruits
fat	supply energy, store fat soluble vitamins	meat, dairy products, oils
iron	promotes health of red blood cells	dark green vegetables, dairy products, meats
water	aids digestion, temperature regulation, alertness	any decaffeinated, low sugar beverage
protein	repairs tissue, provides energy	meat, dairy, legumes, eggs

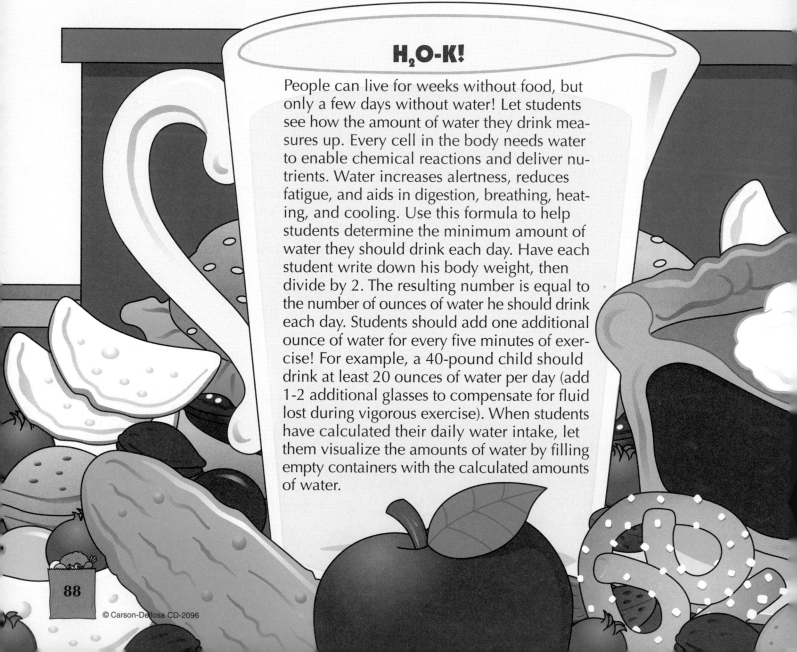

H_2O-K!

People can live for weeks without food, but only a few days without water! Let students see how the amount of water they drink measures up. Every cell in the body needs water to enable chemical reactions and deliver nutrients. Water increases alertness, reduces fatigue, and aids in digestion, breathing, heating, and cooling. Use this formula to help students determine the minimum amount of water they should drink each day. Have each student write down his body weight, then divide by 2. The resulting number is equal to the number of ounces of water he should drink each day. Students should add one additional ounce of water for every five minutes of exercise! For example, a 40-pound child should drink at least 20 ounces of water per day (add 1-2 additional glasses to compensate for fluid lost during vigorous exercise). When students have calculated their daily water intake, let them visualize the amounts of water by filling empty containers with the calculated amounts of water.

Carbohydrates: Fuel for the Body

Carbohydrates are an important power source! Let students make scientific predictions and draw conclusions about carbohydrates—nutrients that give the body energy. Complex carbohydrates like starch must be broken down before their energy can be used, and are found in potatoes and grains. Simple carbohydrates such as glucose are easily-digested sugars found in sweet treats, milk, and fruits. Place bite-size pieces of food from each Food Pyramid category in separate test tubes or clear plastic cups. Tell students that iodine turns blue-black in the presence of starch. Be careful with iodine, because it can stain skin and clothing, and can be toxic if ingested. Have students predict whether or not each food contains starch. Place three drops of iodine on each food. Have students look at the different colors the iodine turns, and determine which foods contain the most and least starch (the darker the iodine, the more starch a food contains).

Fat Finding Fun

Candy bars, french fries, cheeseburgers—all these favorite foods are high in fat! Like the carbohydrate test, there is a simple test students can do to look for fat. Fats are nutrients that contain twice the energy of carbohydrates. Fat is easily stored and helps protect and insulate the body. Explain that *unsaturated* fats are usually liquid at room temperature, and are found mostly in plants. *Saturated* fats are usually solid at room temperature, and can be found in animal products like meat, cheese, and eggs. Saturated fats contain cholesterol, a waxy substance that can build up in blood vessels and cause heart disease. To find fat in foods, cut fruits, vegetables, breads, and cheeses into pieces. Crush pretzels, potato chips, milk chocolate, and nuts. Let students predict which foods contain fat. Cut a brown paper bag into 5" x 5" squares and place each food on a separate square. Allow the foods to stay on the squares for two hours. Explain that foods containing fat will leave an oily, shiny stain on the paper. Have students create graphs showing whether each food contains fat. Remind students that they should eat only the recommended daily allowance of fat, and should eat more unsaturated fats than saturated ones.

Breakfast Brainstorming

Do your students ever wonder why breakfast is the most important meal of the day? Promote healthy breakfasting with problem-solving posters. Explain that "breakfast" is short for "to *break* the *fast*" (a *fast* is a period of time without eating). After going all night without food, our bodies need more fuel. Breakfast increases daily strength, endurance, and alertness. It gives more power to the brain and can even improve your mood! As a class, brainstorm analogies matching this format: [food fuels bodies]. Examples include *gasoline fuels cars*; *electricity powers lights*; etc. Conclude that without breakfast, we would be like cars with no gas! Extend this activity by taking a survey to see how many students eat breakfast. List reasons why people might not eat breakfast. Have students think of solutions to these problems, then draw pictures that promote eating breakfast. Provide muffins and juice and enjoy a class breakfast while students complete the project.

Not Hungry Yet?

Drink milk or juice, or have a bite-sized breakfast!

ON THE GO? EAT A PORTABLE BREAKFAST: FRUITS, VEGGIES, BREAKFAST BARS, OR MUFFINS

Vegetarian Values

Could students give up their fast food cheeseburgers? Tell students that a vegetarian is an individual who chooses not to eat meat. Explain that many vegetarians hope to avoid the risks of cancer, obesity, and heart disease associated with high meat-content diets, while other vegetarians avoid meat out of concern for animals and the environment, or other personal preferences. The strictest vegetarians, *vegans*, do not eat any foods that come from animals, including milk, cheese, and eggs. Give each student a copy of the food pyramid pattern (page 92). Explain that protein is found in many sources other than meat, such as beans, nuts, eggs, milk, and cheese. Provide nutrition information from these products. Challenge students to plan vegetarian breakfast, lunch, and dinner menus which still provide enough protein (2-3 servings per day).

I am a Carrot

I Am a Carrot

Planting seeds of imagination will yield dramatic results. On index cards, write different food items, such as *oranges, peanuts, okra, milk,* etc. (Avoid meat references for this activity.) Let each child choose an index card. Provide books or allow Internet research for students to gather information about how their foods are grown and harvested. Then, let each child write a brief story about the growth, harvest, and preparation of his food—from the food's point of view! Students can design covers for their stories with animated food pictures, then take on the foods' characteristics and give a dramatic reading to the class.

Got Advertising?

Sell the idea of eating well! Let students design and plan a healthy food ad campaign. Ask students to brainstorm their favorite foods and think about the ways those products are advertised— television, radio, magazines, billboards, etc. Assign students to small groups and allow each to choose a healthy food to advertise. Encourage students to create a logo, label, slogan, and/or jingle to promote their products. Have groups script television commercials and radio skits, design billboards on butcher paper, or create magazine ads. Let each group present its ad to the class.

Just the Facts!

Use label logic to understand the nutritional information found on many food labels. Explain that labels allow people to compare ingredients and nutritional content of similar foods. Have students bring food labels to class. Point out the location of the following label information: serving size, nutrients (fat, cholesterol, sodium, fiber, protein, etc.) per serving, and the percentage of the daily recommended value of nutrients per serving. Let students use this information to compare labels and answer questions such as, *Which food contains the most Vitamin C?*, *Which food has the smallest serving size?*, *Which food is lowest in sodium content?*, *Which food provides the highest percentage of total carbohydrates?*, etc.

Play with Food

Let students observe, celebrate, and enjoy the wonders of food! In a large box at the front of the room, provide a variety of ready-to-eat "whole" foods, such as oranges, nuts, apples, bananas, carrots, grapes, pretzels, etc. Assign each child a number, then have him write his number on a slip of paper. Collect the slips and place them in a jar. Call out the numbers as you draw them out one by one. As each child's name is called, have him choose a food from the box. Instruct students not to eat their foods! Let students "play with" their foods, writing vivid descriptions of how their foods smell, feel, and taste. Let each child research and record the nutritional value of his food, then illustrate the food on the same paper as the food observations.

91

blank food pyramid

vegetables

milk, yogurt, cheese

fats, oils, sweets

bread, cereal, rice, pasta

fruits

meat, beans, eggs, nuts

food pyramid

COPY and CUT

92

© Carson-Dellosa CD-2096

INTERNATIONAL Holidays

Holi

Holi (HOE•lee) or *Holika*, also known as the Festival of Colors, is a Hindu holiday that occurs in early March. Signifying the arrival of spring and the passing of winter, Holi marks the triumph of good over evil. Legend has it that a tyrannical king wanted everyone to worship him. His son, Prahlad (pra•LAHD), refused and the king was angered. Prahlad was cast into a fire but survived because of his religious faith. Today, people celebrate by lighting bonfires the night before Holi. The next day, people smear each other with colorful powder called *gulal* (goo•LAL) and throw colored water.

We Can All Get Along

One reason for throwing colored powders and water on Holi is to bring equality to people. The powder symbolizes equality, because everyone looks the same. All barriers are knocked down on this holiday and everyone gets along. Have students celebrate this aspect of Holi. As a class, brainstorm a list of possible conflicts and resolutions. Then, have each student illustrate one concept and write a short paragraph about it. Let each student present his illustration to the class. After everyone has made a presentation, hang the illustrations with the other Holi crafts on a bulletin board titled *Working Toward Peace*.

Oh, Colorful You!

Show students how colorful they are! When Hindus smear powder on each other, it is known as *playing Holi*. Let students play Holi without getting their clothes messy! Pair students and give each student a large sheet of butcher paper. Have each student trace the other's body outline on the paper. Tell students to write their names on the outlines and trade with another student. Next, provide dry tempera paint, water, and paint brushes. Then, have each student dip a brush into the water, then into the powder, and paint inside the outline. Popular powder colors used during Holi are green, pink, orange, yellow, red, and blue. Hang the completed shapes in the classroom as a colorful reminder of Holi.

Holi (continued)

Clearly Colorful

Turn ordinary water into a rainbow of colors! Make different colored dyes by bringing in parts of plants and flowers. Red onion skins make red dye, marigold flowers make brown dye, yellow onion peels make yellow dye and moss makes green dye. For each color, boil four cups of water, add the plants (color will vary according to how much is added), and simmer for 15 minutes. Provide paint brushes and pieces of cloth and let students carefully paint pictures of Hindu letters or designs on the cloth with the dyes. Display the completed pictures on a bulletin board.

Spray Away!

Budding artists will enjoy this activity! Gather several spray bottles and pour water and a few drops of food coloring in each. Take students outside and place large sheets of white butcher paper on the ground. Let students take turns spraying patterns on the paper. Let the paint dry, then take the papers inside and hang them in the classroom.

Sweet Eats

Prepare sweet treats for everyone! During Holi it is customary to eat yellow candies called *laddu* (lad•DOO) which are made from split pea flour and sugar syrup. Make treats to represent laddu with this recipe.

Ingredients:
1/4 cup margarine
10-ounce package mini marshmallows
6 cups rice cereal
1 tablespoon yellow food coloring

Melt the margarine in a deep pan over low heat. Add the marshmallows and stir until completely melted. Remove from heat and add the rice cereal and food coloring. Stir until the cereal is coated with the mixture. Press the mixture into a buttered 9" x 13" pan. When the mixture is cool, let each student grab a small amount and roll it into a ball. Provide yellow plastic wrap for students to wrap the treats in to take home, or allow students to eat laddu for a snack.

Purim

Purim (POO•rim) is a Jewish holiday occurring in the month of *Adar* (a•DAR), which falls in February or March. It is a joyous occasion when Queen Esther is celebrated for saving Jews in ancient Persia from a villainous man named Haman (HAY•men). Children dress in costumes and perform plays of the Purim story. Many families go to a special service at the synagogue in which the book of Esther is read. After the service, people gather for a huge feast, which includes meat and pastries.

Rattle Haman!

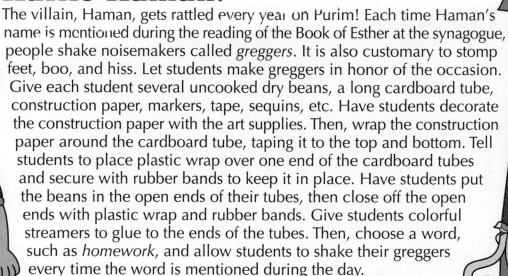

The villain, Haman, gets rattled every year on Purim! Each time Haman's name is mentioned during the reading of the Book of Esther at the synagogue, people shake noisemakers called *greggers*. It is also customary to stomp feet, boo, and hiss. Let students make greggers in honor of the occasion. Give each student several uncooked dry beans, a long cardboard tube, construction paper, markers, tape, sequins, etc. Have students decorate the construction paper with the art supplies. Then, wrap the construction paper around the cardboard tube, taping it to the top and bottom. Tell students to place plastic wrap over one end of the cardboard tubes and secure with rubber bands to keep it in place. Have students put the beans in the open ends of their tubes, then close off the open ends with plastic wrap and rubber bands. Give students colorful streamers to glue to the ends of the tubes. Then, choose a word, such as *homework*, and allow students to shake their greggers every time the word is mentioned during the day.

Haman's Ears

Treat students to these yummy pastries. During Purim, people eat special pastries called *Hamantashen* (HAH•man•tash•in), which are said to represent the ears of Haman. Make a batch of these yummy desserts to share.

Hamantashen Ingredients

2/3 cup butter
1/2 cup sugar
1 egg
1/4 cup orange juice without pulp

1 cup white flour
1 cup wheat flour
various preserves

Blend the butter and sugar. Add egg and blend. Add orange juice and blend. Add flour, 1/2 cup at a time, alternating between white and wheat, blending each thoroughly. Refrigerate the batter overnight. Roll the dough thinly between two pieces of waxed paper lightly dusted with white flour. Cut out 3" circles. Put preserves in the middle of each circle. Fold the sides to make a triangle, overlapping them so a little filling shows through the middle. Squeeze the corners firmly, so they do not come apart while baking. Bake at 375° for 10-15 minutes or until golden brown. Makes about 20 pastries.

Purim (continued)

Sweet Gift Boxes

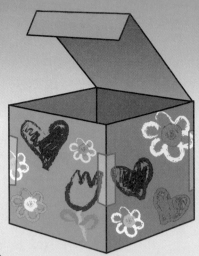

It is customary for children to make gift boxes, fill them with fruit or candy, and give them to friends during Purim. The giving of gifts on Purim is known as *Mishloach Manot* (mish•lo•AK mah•NOTE). Let students participate in this custom by making their own gift boxes with sweet treats for friends or family members. Create a box pattern on paper for each student as shown in the diagram (left). Have her decorate it. Fold up the edges, tape the sides together, and fold down the top. Give each student several small candies, such as jelly beans, chocolates, etc., to put in the box. Allow students to give the boxes as gifts.

Who Are You?

What do Purim and costume parties have in common? Costumes! Children wear costumes on Purim because a verse in the Torah states *And I shall surely hide My face on that day* (Dvarim 31). Let students join in the fun by making their own costumes to disguise their identities! Provide construction paper, cardboard, grocery bags, crayons, markers, etc., and let students make their own costumes. Hats can be made from construction paper, shirts can be made from paper grocery bags, etc. Let each student stand in front of the class while others try to guess who he is and what his costume is. When everyone has had a turn, let students parade around the room!

It's Time for Jokes

Because Purim is one of the most festive holidays on the Jewish calendar, it is also a time for jokes. This custom is based on the phrase *Venahafoch hu* (ven•ah•HA•fak hue), which means *the opposite happened*. The phrase is found in the Megillat (meh•GE•latt) Esther, (the scroll of Esther). Let students write their own jokes to celebrate. Give each student a piece of paper and have her draw and color a door. Then, have students cut out the top, bottom, and right sides of the doors, so that the doors opens. Let each child write a knock knock joke on or above the door, with the punch line on the inside of the door. Bind the pages into a class book titled *Someone's at the Door!* Let students take turns taking the book home to share with family members.

Knock knock!
Who's there?
Canoe!
Canoe who?
Canoe come out and play?

To Peach
    July 4, 1991
To Paul
    August 17, 1991

Hope it's helpful and fun
all my love Marie

1 0 0
GOLFING
TIPS

1 0 0
GOLFING
TIPS

RICHARD BRADBEER · IAN MORRISON

THE
APPLE
PRESS

A QUINTET BOOK

Published by The Apple Press
6 Blundell Street, London N7 9BH

ISBN 1-85076-242-2

This book was designed and produced by
Quintet Publishing Limited
6 Blundell Street
London N7 9BH

Creative Director: Peter Bridgewater
Art Director: Ian Hunt
Designer: Stuart Walden
Project Editor: Shaun Barrington
Photographer: Ian Howes

Typeset in Great Britain by
Central Southern Typesetters, Eastbourne
Manufactured in Hong Kong by
Regent Publishing Services Limited
Printed in Hong Kong by
Leefung-Asco Printers Limited

**Directional instructions
throughout assume that the
player is right-handed.**

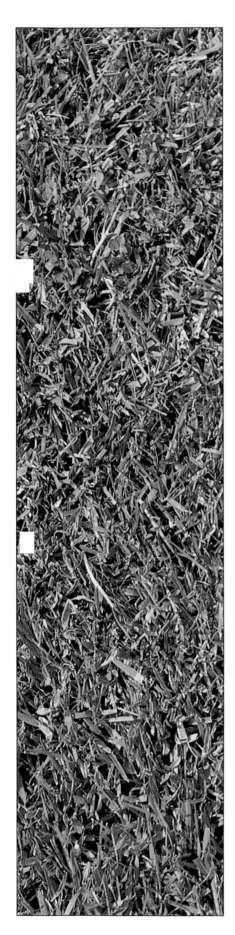

. . . .
CONTENTS
. . . .

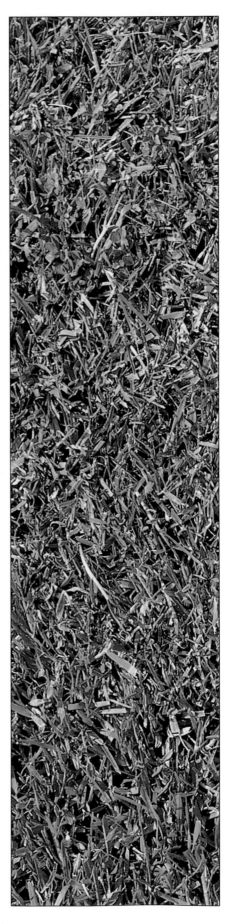

1

THE DEMANDS OF GOLF

There are many people who believe that golf is a good form of exercise and is a way of keeping you fit. Certainly it will not do you any harm, but in order to play good golf you need to be fit in the first place. In fact, physical fitness is only one of the demands the game of golf puts on you. The others are the *mental* and *enviromental* demands.

Golf needs intense concentration; that is one of the mental demands. It can also be a frustrating game at times. That is another mental demand. You should be ready for both during the course of a game.

Golf is a great 'leveller'. Because of the handicapping system, golfers of different standards can compete on level terms. If you are a low handicap player you are expected to win a lot. But if for some reason you are suddenly not winning regularly, then you have to cope with the situation. Probably you will need to go back to something elementary, like your hold, or stance, or swing. But being able to look for faults is proof that you can cope with the enviromental demands of the game.

2

WARMING UP: 1

You should never go into any sporting exercise without first warming up. A cold body will not respond well and that principle also applies to golf.

While you are waiting on the tee, or before you reach the teeing ground, do a couple of limbering up exercises to get the blood flowing through the muscles you are about to use.

Simulated golf swings with one, two or even three clubs in your hand, will certainly help as will the exercise shown, which will help to loosen up your back muscles and improve suppleness.

If you were a sprinter, or footballer, you would make sure you were warmed up before you raced or started your game. Golf is no different.

Place the club across your shoulder blades, holding it in place with your arms

Now complete a full turn of the body in the backswing

RIGHT Swing back rhythmically and gently to the follow-through position

Lean forward from the waist to the address position. Hold the club in the middle, hands about a foot apart

Swing back to shoulder level

Swing through, again to shoulder level

3
· · · ·
WARMING UP: 2
· · · ·

This is another simple exercise you can carry out while waiting on the tee. Again it helps to loosen up the leg, arm and back muscles, and simulates the golf swing at the same time.

4
· · · ·
GETTING TO KNOW YOUR CLUB
· · · ·

You will be familiar with the various parts of the golf club; the handle, the shaft and the clubhead. But the part you will not be as familiar with, and probably the most important part of the club is the **leading edge.**

When many novices line up the clubhead up with the ball they often do so with the top of the club face. This is incorrect. It is the bottom of the club face which should be lined up. And it is that part of the club which is known as the leading edge.

At all times the leading edge should be at right angles to the ball and ball-to-target line. You may play some shots with an 'open' or 'closed' club face, but at contact the leading edge will still be square to the ball and ball-to-target line.

To appreciate the leading edge, stand opposite a player who

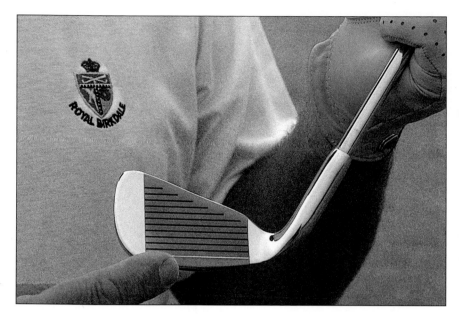

TOP RIGHT Leading edge square to the ball-to-target line

BELOW The lie of a driver, compared to a short iron

has adopted a normal stance. You can now see the leading edge of the club at right-angles to the ball-to-target line. Keep your eye on the clubhead as it is taken into its backswing. The face of the club will begin to look larger to you, the onlooker. And as it returns to make contact with the ball the face appears to get smaller and the leading edge becomes apparent once more. As the club goes into the follow-through position, note how the back of the club face starts to become more visible.

This forms the basis of the golf swing. It is your blueprint. Remember there is only one contact between golf club and golf ball, and that is with the leading edge square to the ball-to-target line.

5
· · · ·
NOT ALL CLUBS ARE THE SAME ...
· · · ·

A quick look will tell you that golf clubs are very different. Some are woods, some irons and, of course, the putter is different again. You will also notice at a glance that they are of different lengths. The higher the club number gets, the shorter it is in length. The higher the club number, the more acute the angle of loft on the club face gets.

But an important aspect of the differences between golf clubs, which many novices ignore, is the different lie of each club which makes a difference to the swing path.

So it is important to realize at this stage that clubs are not only of different loft and length, but also have different lies.

6

UNDERSTANDING AIM

Many players, escpecially novices, will often believe they are aiming their club and ball in the correct direction when, in reality, it is either too far to the right, or left, of the target.

You must firstly identify the ball-to-target line, which is the imaginary line drawn between your ball and the target. Your feet should then be in line with that imaginary line and the leading edge of your club should be square to the ball and the line.

To establish the ball-to-target line, stand directly behind your ball and draw that imaginary line in your mind. Try picking out a landmark about 10ft in front of your ball which is in line between the ball and target, and use that as a guide for establishing your correct ball-to-target line.

The red flag is the target here. Check your body alignment by setting one club across the line of your toes and aiming at the target. Place another just inside the ball, parallel with the first club. Set another club between your feet, just inside your left heel with the grip just reaching the ball. This must be at right angles to the target line

7
. . . .
CHECKING YOUR AIM
. . . .

Aim, like hold, is one of the basics of golf. Get your grip wrong and you are going to encounter all sorts of problems. And if you don't aim in the right direction, then, how can you realistically expect the ball to go where you want it?

It is surprising how many novice golfers think they are aiming in the right direction. But when you analyze their aim, it is well off-target.

To appreciate aim, you must first understand what is meant by the ball-to-target line. Draw an imaginary line from your ball to its intended target, whether it be a flagstick or some point on the fairway, that imaginary line is the ball-to-target line. To aim correctly, the leading edge of your club should be at right angles to the ball and ball-to-target line. If it is, then your aim is correct.

After setting your club in position on the ground, visually check by looking between the clubhead and target a couple of times to make sure your aim is correct. Don't take it for granted that your aim is correct, even the best players don't do that. You should constantly check your aim. Any slight error will cause the ball to veer away from its intended target.

Watch the flight of your ball to see what your regular flight path is. You can then allow for this when you take aim

8
. . . .
UNDERSTANDING BALL FLIGHT
. . . .

Ball flight is simply what it says and describes the flight the golf ball takes after you hit it. The **straight** flight does, as its name implies, see the ball travel in a straight line.

The scourge of the high-handicap golfer is either the **slice** or the **hook,** which are flight paths, arising from errors.

The slice sees the ball start its journey heading to the left then veering to the right. The hook is the opposite.

Two other flights are the **push** and **pull.** Like the slice and hook they go out to the right and left accordingly, but in both cases the ball doesn't start its travels by going the opposite way first.

Finally, the other two flight paths are the **draw** and **fade.** The former is a shot that sees the golf ball travel out to the right slightly before returning to the target. The fade is the opposite.

11

9
. . . .
OPEN AND CLOSED CLUBHEADS
. . . .

Every golf shot is made with the leading edge of the club square to the ball-to-target line. Don't forget that. Occasionally, you will hear commentators say; 'he played that with an open (or closed) club face'. The club face is *never* actually opened or closed. Your stance creates a so-called 'open' or 'closed' club face but contact is still with the **leading edge square to the ball-to-target line.**

A closed clubhead is one with the leading edge pointing to the left of the ball-to-target line, while an open clubhead points to the right of the ball-to-target line. The correct position should be square.

An open or closed club face will seriously affect the flight of the ball. The most common cause of the club face being opened or closed is because of an incorrect grip.

TOP LEFT This picture shows the open club face

ABOVE An open clubface

ABOVE The cubface here is already slightly closed. Imagine its position by the time it reaches the front ball

ABOVE A closed clubface

12

10
· · · ·
THE HOLD – THE LEFT HAND
· · · ·

TOP LEFT This is the correct position of the club across the left hand

ABOVE View of the correct left hand hold from a chest-on viewpoint

The hold, more commonly, but incorrectly, called the 'grip', is a crucial aspect of golf. Get the hold wrong and you can expect all sorts of problems.

The left hand is the most dominant of the two hands when adopting your hold, but you do not grip the club with all four fingers and thumb of the hand. Only the first three fingers are used.

To grip the club correctly place the club diagonally across the palm of your left hand and apply pressure with the first three fingers. The thumb and index finger are to be used for support only; not for gripping the handle of the club.

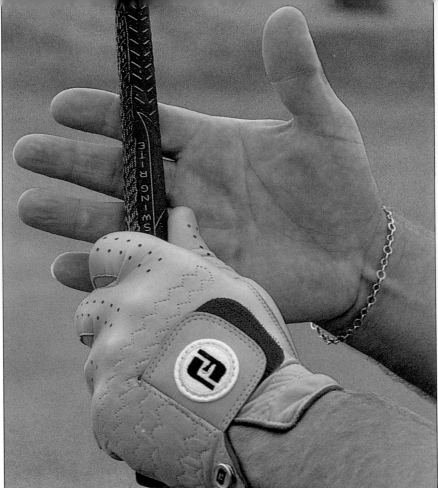

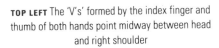

11
. . . .
THE HOLD – THE RIGHT HAND
. . . .

Having correctly placed the club in the left hand, now place the right hand on the club but apply pressure with the second and third fingers only. All other fingers are for support. You should adopt any one of the three standard holds. Each is designed to accommodate hands of various shapes and sizes. The grips are so designed for personal comfort, no other reason. Why not try all three to see how comfortable (or uncomfortable) you feel with each? There will be one to suit your needs.

Irrespective of which hold you adopt, you must make sure that your hands are kept as close together as possible and that the little finger of your left hand is approximately one inch from the top of the handle. It is also important that both your hands work together as one unit.

To check that you are holding the club correctly, place the club-head on the floor in the address position. The 'V's formed by the index finger and thumb of each hand should *both* be pointing to a point midway between your head and right shoulder. This rule applies no matter which club you are using. If you are having problems with your swing at any time, check your hold, it could be that's where your problems are starting.

12

. . . .

ADOPTING THE OVERLAPPING HOLD

. . . .

Commonly referred to as the Vardon grip, the overlapping hold is named after the six-times winner of the British Open, Harry Vardon, who is widely reported to have been the first man to use it. It is regarded as the standard hold and is the most popular of the three holds.

The little finger of your right hand (if you are right-handed) rests on top of the forefinger of your left hand.

It is important with the overlapping hold, and with other types of holds mentioned for full shots that the 'V' formed by the thumb and forefinger of each hand points in the same direction, ie to a point between your face and right shoulder.

13

. . . .

ADOPTING THE INTERLOCKING HOLD

. . . .

The interlocking grip is very little different to the overlapping hold, but this time the forefinger of the gloved hand and the little finger of your right hand overlap. This grip is ideal for lady golfers or male players with small hands.

BOTTOM LEFT The overlapping hold

BOTTOM RIGHT The interlocking hold

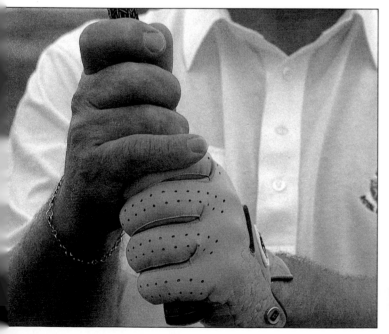

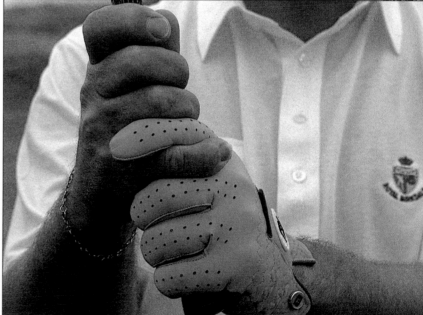

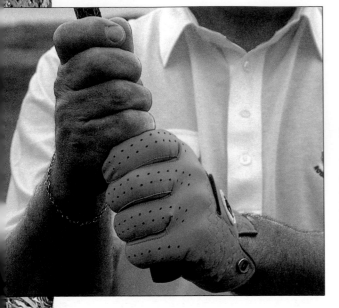

ABOVE The two-handed hold, with every finger on the handle

FAR RIGHT A relaxed address position. There should be no feeling of tension

14
· · · ·
ADOPTING THE TWO-HANDED HOLD
· · · ·

This is the least used of all holds but is one adopted by people who are unable to put a strong hold on the handle. As you will see, all your fingers and thumbs come into contact with the club handle. It is similar to the hold a baseball player would have on his bat. It is also sometimes referred to as the double-handed grip.

15
· · · ·
ADDRESSING THE BALL
· · · ·

The ball position in relation to your feet is important. For woods and longer irons it should be level with your left heel. But as the club gets shorter then the position of the ball moves to a point midway between your two feet.

To make sure your address is correct, line up the leading edge of your club with the ball and ball-to-target line. Then adopt your normal hold. You should now be in the correct address position.

16
· · · ·
RELAX AT ADDRESS
· · · ·

Many golfers, as soon as they stand on the tee and address the ball, suddenly feel a tenseness run through their body. This happens to the novice quite often on the first tee when there is a great deal of pressure on him to 'get the ball away'. A tense body does nothing for the smooth rhythm of the swing.

The tension often starts in the hands and spreads throughout the body. Check that you are not gripping the club too tightly. You need a firm, but not over-tight, grip. If you are conscious that you are gripping too tightly then let go of the club, step back from the ball, and start all over again. It is amazing just how much this can help.

17

· · · ·

POSITIONING THE BALL IN RELATION TO YOUR FEET

· · · ·

When playing a shot, the position of the ball will be dictated by the length of club being used. When using a driver, for example, the ball will be positioned at a point level with your left heel. But as the club gets shorter, to say a 9-iron, the ball position will move away from your left foot to a position between your two feet.

18

· · · ·

HOW HIGH TO TEE THE BALL

· · · ·

The only advice on this subject is to make sure that, with woods, at least half the ball is visible over the top of the club face at address. But don't tee it up too high. The size of the club face will therefore dictate how high you tee-up your ball.

You wouldn't tee the ball this high when using an iron club off the tee. In fact, you don't have to tee your ball on a teeing peg. At

TOP LEFT Ball position for the driver

ABOVE For a 9-iron, the ball is further back, almost to the midway point between the feet

RIGHT About half the ball is visible above the face of this wooden club

short holes the more experienced golfers prefer to play the ball off the ground so as to improve the chance of imparting backspin on the ball. However, as a matter of etiquette, and so as not to cause damage to the teeing ground, you are advised to use a teeing peg at all times.

Don't forget, you aren't allowed to tee up your ball on the fairway, only on the teeing ground. In winter months most courses allow 'preferred lies' to protect the course, but this doesn't mean you can take out a tee and tee up your ball!

TOP LEFT Bend forward from the hips for the address position. Your knees should only bend enough to avoid stiffness

ABOVE A chest-on view of the address position

19
. . . .
THE CORRECT POSTURE
. . . .

One of the biggest faults of the high-handicap player is the bending of his, or her, knees too much.

The most important thing to remember about correct posture is adopting the correct angle of your spine. To establish this, stand upright and bend your back slightly forward so that your hips and rear-end stick out just slightly. Then flex your knees inward towards each other.

You must maintain this spinal angle throughout your golf swing.

ABOVE When you hold your left arm straight down your side, the club forms an angle

TOP RIGHT At address there isn't a straight line between club and arm to the shoulder

20
. . . .
SETTING THE CORRECT LEFT ARM POSITION
. . . .

Many novices think the left arm and club have to be straight as one unit. This is not the case. Try holding your left arm straight down by your side and put a club in your hand and try to maintain it as one straight unit. The only way you can do so is by tilting your body to the right. That is not a natural stance for anything, let alone playing golf.

You must keep your left arm straight when swinging a golf club but to appreciate what this really means, hold your arm down by your side and open your fingers slightly and insert any club. You will now see that the club is at an angle. You will also see that your left arm *is* straight. That is the correct and natural way to hold a golf club. When you adopt your stance at address you should maintain that hold, don't try to make the point between the clubhead and your shoulder one continuous line.

If you look at the handle of your club you will note a pattern. This is there to help you to ensure your hands are lined up with the leading edge.

TOP LEFT When club and left arm are in a straight line, a cramped shoulder position is the result

ABOVE In this address position the shoulders remain cramped

BELOW The right shoulder is naturally lower than the left

21

. . . .

THE INCORRECT LEFT ARM POSITION

. . . .

See what happens when the left arm is kept straight and rigid? The left arm is elevated far too much and the entire body looks tense. When we say 'keep a straight left arm' it means at the top of the back swing, *not* in the address position.

22

. . . .

SHOULDER POSITION AT THE ADDRESS

. . . .

Having adopted a good posture with a perfect spinal angle you will now be in such a position that you can make at least a complete 90° shoulder turn, which is crucial to the full golf shot. When you take up your correct address your right shoulder should be slightly lower than your left.

   If you turn your shoulders through a complete 90°, your hips will turn through 45°.

ABOVE The head is slightly behind the ball

BELOW The head remains in the same position at the top of the backswing. It shouldn't be pulled further to your right

BOTTOM RIGHT The head is still behind the ball just after impact

23
· · · ·
HEAD POSITION AT THE ADDRESS
· · · ·

Except when putting, when your head is directly over the ball, it should at all other times be slightly behind the ball. If it is not, then you are stretching, which means your swing will be un-balanced and consequently a whole host of problems are in store. So, keep your head *slightly* behind the ball.

24
· · · ·
HEAD POSITION – IN THE BACKSWING AND AT IMPACT
· · · ·

Note how, throughout the swing the head remains in the same position at the backswing and even at impact is still behind the ball. This is a very important point to remember when playing the golf shot, keep your head behind the ball.

25

· · · ·

YOUR WRISTS: THE SHORT GAME

· · · ·

In most golf shots your wrists 'cock' as part of the stroke. The point of the backswing when they actually 'cock' depends upon the club being used.

When playing the short game, ie when using the short irons, then they cock earlier than with the long irons or woods.

BELOW LEFT Early wrist cock when playing a short iron

ABOVE With a long iron, the wrists should cock much later

26

· · · ·

YOUR WRISTS: THE LONG GAME

· · · ·

With long irons and woods the wrists don't cock until nearly at the top of the back swing. The simple rule to remember is: the shorter the club, the earlier the wrists 'cock'.

ABOVE The insides of the feet are at shoulder width for playing a wood

TOP RIGHT The stance narrows as the clubs get shorter

27

· · · ·

THE CORRECT WIDTH OF STANCE

· · · ·

There is no hard-and-fast rule over how far you should have your feet apart. Your choice of club and, of course, your own personal physique, will play an important part in such a decision.

However, as a general guideline your feet should be a shoulder-width apart, and measured to the inside of your shoes when playing with woods. As the clubs get shorter then the outside of your shoes should be level with your shoulders.

Another important feature of the stance are your knees: keep them very slightly bent inward towards each other. This way they are in the 'ready' position and all set to play their part in the swing.

28

. . . .

ADOPTING A SQUARE STANCE

. . . .

When taking up a square stance your feet should be parallel to the ball-to-target line. Your right foot will be at 90° to it, while your left foot will be pointing at a slight angle of about 15°.

29

. . . .

OPEN AND CLOSED STANCES

. . . .

When an open stance is adopted the line of the feet, knees, hips, and shoulders will aim to the left of your target line. When a closed (or shut) stance is adopted, the line of the feet, knees, hips, and shoulders will aim to the right of the target line.

ABOVE Feet parallel to the target line

BOTTOM LEFT Closed stance

BELOW Open stance

30

UNDERSTANDING SWING PATH

The entire left side of the body moves to the right in one piece

Firstly you must understand what is meant by **Outside** and **Inside.**

If you adopt your normal stance your feet are positioned on the **Inside** of the ball-to-target line. The area the other side of the line is known as **Outside.**

A normal golf stroke is played with an **inside-to-square** swing path. In other words, the clubhead is taken back on the inside, makes contact with the ball, and follows through on the inside.

A swing that sees the clubhead taken away on the outside and follows through on the inside, after making contact, is known as the **out-to-in** swing path. And a clubhead taken away on the inside and following through on the outside is known as an **in-to-out** swing path.

Remember these three swing paths: we will come across them quite a lot when looking at faults and their causes later on. Often problems are caused by an incorrect swing path.

31

THE TAKEAWAY

The takeaway is the first action in the golf swing. So make sure you get it right. If you don't then you cannot expect the clubhead to be in the right place at impact.

It is a one-piece movement and the entire left side of your body, including the shaft and clubhead, move towards your right side. This is all made possible because your right hip and shoulder move backward slightly.

However, it is important to make sure your hands and wrist maintain their shape and that your elbows remain a constant distance apart throughout the takeaway and the rest of the swing.

We said earlier that the leading edge must be square to the ball and ball-to-target line, and indeed it will be as you address the ball. But as you begin the takeaway it will no longer be square to the ball-to-target line. Don't worry, if you carry out the rest of the swing correctly it will be square when it returns to its impact position.

32
· · · ·
THE BACKSWING
· · · ·

TOP LEFT The left arm is comfortably – not rigidly – straight

ABOVE The clubhead has crossed the target line

FACING PAGE, TOP LEFT The club is in a flat, or laid-off position

FACING PAGE, TOP RIGHT The club is parallel with the target line

It is so important that after a smooth takeaway you now take the club into its backswing with a fluent and continuous movement of your upper body as your arms take the club above your head.

The backswing depends upon so many factors: you should make sure your wrists 'cock' naturally and that you keep your left arm straight. It doesn't have to be rigidly straight. It must, however, be comfortable.

At the top of the backswing your right elbow should be pointing at the ground slightly behind your right heel and the shaft of the club should be parallel to the ball-to-target line. And finally, you should have maintained you elbows at the same distance apart throughout the backswing; they should be the same distance apart at the top of the backswing as they were at the address. The club should be parallel to the ball-to-target line at the top of the back swing and *not* across the line or laid off.

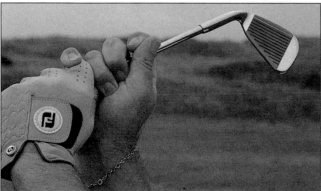

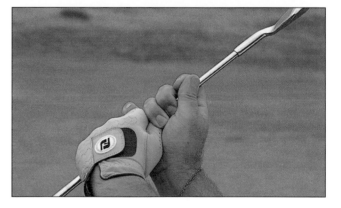

CENTRE LEFT Grip down the shaft to
see that your clubhead is reaching the correct
position at the top. This is fine, with the toe of the
club pointing towards the target

CENTRE RIGHT Here the clubface is shut

BOTTOM LEFT Now the clubface is open

33
· · · ·
THE DOWNSWING
· · · ·

From the top of your backswing you have now to bring the club back to its original position. This part of the swing is the downswing and is crucial.

Everything must come back down just as it went up, and in one complete unit. If it didn't then you can't expect your clubhead to be square to the ball and ball-to-target line at impact.

The hips play an important role in the downswing and they move slightly ahead of the hands as your weight is transferred to your left leg, enabling you to keep your body square at impact. It is important that you keep a steady head and maintain your correct spinal angle.

FACING PAGE, TOP LEFT Hips have returned to the address position while the hands are still above waist level

FACING PAGE, BOTTOM LEFT Weight is now almost entirely on the left side at this point

FACING PAGE, BOTTOM RIGHT A well-balanced finish to the through-swing

BOTTOM LEFT Feet and legs at the top of the backswing

BOTTOM CENTRE Feet and legs at impact

BOTTOM RIGHT Feet and legs for the through-swing

34

· · · ·

THE FOLLOW THROUGH

· · · ·

The action of the club following through will automatically bring your head up eventually, so don't be tempted to lift it early.

Once the clubhead has made contact with the ball, allow it to continue its swing so that it will end up behind your head. As it pulls upward after impact it will not only lift your head for you, but your weight will be transferred to your left leg and your right leg will be bent at the knee, with your right foot resting on the toe of your shoe.

35

· · · ·

CORRECT LEG POSITONS

· · · ·

At the top of the backswing your weight should be transferred to your right leg and your left knee bent inwards. On impact, the weight will have transferred to your left leg and your right knee will now be bent inward. As the swing is completed and you go into your follow-through position, your right knee will be pointing at the target and your right leg will be supported on your toes. The left foot will be slightly bent over onto its side.

36

· · · ·

KEEPING YOUR EYE ON THE BALL

· · · ·

Keeping your eye on the ball is a great adage adopted in all ball games. But, when playing the full golf shot, you actually keep your eye trained on the *back* of the ball.

37

· · · ·

MAINTAINING YOUR BALANCE

· · · ·

Good balance is crucial to the golf swing. Overbalancing often occurs when you try to hit the ball too hard and become more physical in your approach. To test your balance, try holding your follow-through position until your ball has landed. If you can, then your balance is alright.

ABOVE Try to hold that follow-through position to test your balance

Make sure the clubhead sits nicely on the fairway and lines up correctly with the ball

38

· · · ·

PLAYING FAIRWAY WOODS

· · · ·

This shot is often the one that most novices dread. But why should they? The wood is no different to any other club in your bag, just a little longer. Once you have mastered your grip, stance and swing, then playing with a wooden club off the fairway should pose no problems.

Conditions and lie of the ball dictate whether you should attempt a wood off the fairway. But if you have a good lie, then take a wooden club out of your bag. Don't, however, attempt a driver off the fairway, leave that to the experts. Instead, use a more lofted wooden club, like a 2-, 3- 4- or 5-wood.

You want to make sure that the leading edge of your club (remember it is the bottom of the club face) sits nicely on the ground. If it doesn't, then you have probably taken the wrong club and are well advised to look at the alternative of playing an iron.

Move your left foot nearer the target line in order
to close the stance

39
. . . .
CLOSE YOUR STANCE WHEN
USING A WOOD
. . . .

Because of the length of the wooden clubs and long irons, it is a good tip to adopt a slightly closed stance when playing a shot with one of these clubs.

With the club being longer you need to get your right shoulder out of the way during the swing. A slightly closed stance will help you to pivot better.

Playing with long irons – your shoulders should be
level with the inside of your heels

40

· · · ·

PLAYING WITH LONG IRONS

· · · ·

You must appreciate that as club numbers get higher the length
of the club gets shorter. Consequently it is impossible to adopt the
same stance for every club. When you place a 1-iron on the ground
you will notice how much flatter than a 9-iron it is. You have to
make the necessary adjustment in your stance.

The long irons are those often referred to as the 1-, 2-, 3- and 4-
irons. Because they are still regarded as the 'long clubs' you have

to play them with a full swing just as you would if you were playing a wooden club. The ball position varies according to the length of club used. For a 1-iron it will be nearer to a point level with your left heel than with a 4-iron, when it moves to a position toward the midway point between your feet.

When adopting your stance for a long iron, your shoulder should be level with the inside of your heels. Your right foot should be slightly drawn back from the ball to target line, to enable you to get your body into a full swing.

41
· · · ·
PLAYING WITH MEDIUM IRONS
· · · ·

The medium irons are the 5, 6 and 7 irons. Because the length of the club is getting shorter then you should stand nearer to the ball at address and your shoulders should now be level with the outside of your heels.

Your feet, shoulders, knees and hips should now be square to the ball-to-target line. The right foot is not drawn back this time.

Because the club is shorter you adopt a more upright stance and as a result your swing is shorter.

As the ball position is now more towards the middle of your two feet, your head is not as far behind the ball as it was with the driver. But don't be tempted to move it forward; your head should still be behind the ball.

For the medium iron, the ball is further back in the stance and the body is again square to the ball-to-target line

When using the medium irons you are more likely to take divots with your shots; this is because of the upright nature of the swing. Divots are a natural part of the game. You are not doing anything wrong if you take a divot but, whatever you do, please replace the divot after you have played your shot.

42

· · · ·

PLAYING WITH SHORT IRONS

· · · ·

The short irons are the Nos. 8- and 9- irons and the two wedges, the pitching wedge and the sand wedge.

Take hold of a sand wedge and adopt your normal stance. Note where your hands are positioned. Now put it back in your bag and take out your driver and adopt your normal stance and again note where your hands are positioned. In both cases they should be in a position just above your left knee. If they aren't then you have adopted either the wrong hold or body position.

The purpose of this exercise is to show you how some things never change, no matter which club you are playing. All golf shots are the same, it's just that the clubs are of different length and different loft.

The ball position is now at a point midway between your two feet and your left foot should this time be drawn slightly back from the ball-to-target line. The reason for this is because the short iron shot is not played with a full swing, therefore you need to get your body out of the way quickly after making contact. Having your left foot drawn backward enables you to do so. When drawing the left foot back, make sure the shoulders do not move backward at the same time. They should still be parallel to the ball-to-target line.

43

· · · ·

OPEN YOUR STANCE WHEN PLAYING
A SHORT IRON

· · · ·

Because you are not taking a full swing with the shorter irons, the left side of your body will not have time to get out the way as you pivot. Consequently, you need to adopt an open stance which will take your left side away early.

For a short pitch, the ball is almost opposite the right foot and the feet are close together

44
· · · ·
PLAYING THE DRAW AND FADE
· · · ·

There will be times when you will have to play the draw or fade in order to avoid hitting some obstacle, like a tree or bush, that may be in your direct line and thus prevent a straight shot.

The draw is created by a slight **in-to-out** swing path but you must make sure the club face is square to the ball and ball-to-target line at impact. Because the club face is square at impact and the in-to-out swing is adopted, the club causes the ball to travel to the right initially before being drawn back to the target.

The fade is played with a slight out-to-in swing path and, again, with the clubhead square at impact. This time the ball starts off slightly to the left first before veering towards the target.

45
· · · ·
PLAYING THE UPHILL LIE
· · · ·

Sloping lies are not as awkward as most people believe, but they must be played differently to the normal golf shot and you must make some adjustments to your stance and swing.

With the uphill lie you must firstly make sure your body is perpendicular to the ground, just as you would if playing a shot off level ground.

It is crucial that you keep your head position steady. This will make sure the club head swings down and up the slope with a controlled rhythm.

The ball should be slightly forward back at address than it would be for a normal shot with the same club and, because of the lie of the land, a slight **in-to-out** swing path should be adopted. Consequently, the ball will probably be hooked slightly, so aim to the right.

Remember that because the ball is on an upward slope, the slope will help it to take off and get airborne quicker than normal, so you must allow for this by taking a less lofted club, by two if severe, or by one if not so severe. Keep your weight on your right leg so that you can sweep through the ball when making the strike. Keep the backswing short to a maximum of a ¾ swing.

FACING PAGE The blueprint golf swing

A Set the ball a little further back in your stance than for the driver

B One-piece take-away

C The wrists are now cocking

D Full wrist cock at the top of the swing

E Hips lead the downswing

F The ball is on its way and the hands cross over

G Head begins to be pulled round by the shoulders

H Hands are high

I A well-balanced finish

46
· · · ·
PLAYING THE DOWNHILL LIE
· · · ·

There is no denying the downhill lie is one of the most difficult sloping lies to play and it cannot be overstressed how important it is to keep your body perpendicular to the slope throughout the shot. Because you are leaning forward, there is a temptation to move your head too far forward. Be aware of this when taking up your stance.

This time you want to select a club one or two clubs more lofted, depending upon the severity of the slope. If you don't you will lose distance on the shot.

Because the downhill lie has the tendency to create the **out-to-in** swing path you should aim your ball slightly to the left of the target to compensate for the slice. Have the ball slightly back in the address position.

BELOW Allow for less distance from an uphill lie because you will usually get a high trajectory on the ball

BOTTOM RIGHT Swing easily from a downhill lie – it's easy to lose balance

47

. . . .

PLAYING WITH THE BALL BELOW YOUR FEET

. . . .

For this awkward lie, make full use of your club and hold it as near to the butt end of the handle as possible. Position the ball midway between your two feet at address and bend your knees slightly more than usual. The reason for this is to prevent you leaning forward toward the ball which is the natural tendency with such a stance.

An **out-to-in** swing path is likely to be created because, in the downswing, your weight will instinctively shift toward your toes. To compensate for this make sure you aim slightly to the left of the target. Play the shot mainly with hands and arms.

48

. . . .

PLAYING WITH THE BALL ABOVE YOUR FEET

. . . .

The first thing you must do is to shorten the length of your hold on the club handle. Because of the elevation of the land and the slope, you must compensate by making your club 'shorter'.

Position the ball at a point midway between your two feet and aim slightly to the right of the target. Because of your stance and the position of the ball, you will be taking a flatter swing on an **in-to-out** swing path. The result will be a deliberate hook. This is why you need to aim to the right. Again play the shot mainly with hands and arms.

When the ball is below the feet 'lengthen' the club by holding it near the butt

BELOW Well flexed knees help you to maintain balance

49

. . . .

PLAYING OUT OF THE LIGHT ROUGH

. . . .

This is the area between the fairway and the deep rough, or the long grass. While it is not as easy to play out of the light rough as it is from the fairway, it is easier than playing out of deep rough.

Shorter hold when the ball is above the feet

TOP RIGHT Set the weight a little more towards the toes to help balance

However, the one thing that many golfers ignore when they see their ball 'sitting up' in the light rough is the fact that it is sitting up and is resting on top of grass, which is longer than the fairway. When you come to take up your stance your feet will rest on the ground, just as they would on the fairway, but your ball will be 'teed up' slightly. Consequently, if you adopted your normal stance and hold, then the clubhead will travel under the ball instead of making a good contact.

To compensate for this, the answer is simple; shorten the length of your club by moving your hands further down the handle.

50

· · · ·

PLAYING OUT OF LONG GRASS

· · · ·

We have already mentioned ambition, and you are well advised to remember that word when trying to get out of trouble from a lie in long grass.

Firstly, if you analyze your predicament sensibly, you will realize that you have played a bad shot by getting into the grass in the first place, so there is no good reason to believe that you can now play a good shot and play the ball from the rough onto the green. Your best shot may well be with a lofted iron only a few yards

onto the safety of the fairway. If that is the best shot to play, then play it. That is ambition, not over-ambition.

When playing out of long grass, take a heavy club like a wedge. With your ball being buried in grass their will be a tendency for the club shaft to get wrapped up in the grass. Because the wedge has a heavy clubhead it will help make the path to the ball easier.

Take a more upright backswing so you are attacking the ball from an acute angle. Again, this will help to prevent the clubhead getting entangled in the grass. But the most important thing to remember is don't be too ambitious.

TOP LEFT Here the ball is well down in long grass. Use a lofted club to get out

TOP CENTRE Concentrate of making good ball contact

TOP RIGHT The player is well balanced here. He hasn't made the mistake of hitting flat out in the hope of greater distance

51
· · · ·
THE DIFFERENCE BETWEEN PITCHING AND CHIPPING
· · · ·

The **pitch** is played with a lofted club high into the air so that it lands on the green. Depending on the conditions of the ground and weather conditions, the ball may stop dead on landing or roll forward. It may even roll backward if a great deal of backspin has been imparted on the ball and/or conditions facilitate such a shot.

The **chip** is played with a less lofted club and the ball is chipped into the air before running on to its target.

52
. . . .
WHEN TO CHIP OR TO PITCH?
. . . .

Only you can make that decision. Obviously the lie of your ball and local conditions will help with your decision-making. If you are on the fairway with a steep bunker to an elevated green in front of you, then you are left with no alternative but to play the lofted pitch shot. But if you are just off the edge of the green with a clear run to the hole then a chip and run is your best shot. But you must always bear in mind conditions on the course. A wet fairway and green will lend itself to the pitch whereas a dry and rock-hard green is not the best surface to pitch to. In the latter case the chip would be better.

Don't forget also that wind affects the pitch because of the elevated loft of the ball. Lush grass is an ideal surface from which to pitch.

53
. . . .
PITCHING
. . . .

Pitching, like chipping, is that part of the game referred to as the short **game.** The pitch is played with a lofted club which projects the ball high into the air before landing on or near its intended target. It is a shot played with the hands and arms; a full rotation of the body is not necessary.

The key point to remember about pitching is to take less than a full swing of the club because the distance the ball travels is normally a short one.

You should adopt your normal hold on the club and make sure the leading edge is square to the ball and ball-to-target line. Make sure the ball is positioned slightly left of centre at address and keep your shoulders square to the ball-to-target line, but open your stance slightly by drawing back your left foot from the ball-to-target line.

You want to shift slightly more of your bodyweight on to your left leg than you would for a medium or long iron shot. As the downswing commences make sure even more weight is shifted to your left leg.

For delicate short pitch shots to the green move your hands

TOP The ball is well back in the stance. The descending blow will increase backspin

This is the length of swing needed for a short pitch

44

TOP The ball is beginning to climb steeply

Weight is well over to the left side

down the handle of the club to shorten it. For full pitches, hold the club near the top of the handle. Your follow through should be at least as long as your backswing. Finally, don't be afraid to use your sand wedge off the fairway.

54
· · · ·
GETTING THE BALL TO STOP AFTER PITCHING TO THE GREEN
· · · ·

Only the very best of players can get the ball to stop on pitching, but even they cannot do it all the time. A rock-hard green will not lend itself to such a shot, no matter how good the player is.

Top players can manipulate the ball by applying backspin but this requires the very best of contacts between club face and ball. Don't expect every one of your pitches to stop dead; they won't. You must remember that important word 'ambition' which we have used before. If you can pitch to the green and get yourself in a position for a single putt then you will have achieved your goal. Don't expect the ball to stop dead six inches from the hole every time.

55
· · · ·
A FINAL TIP ON PITCHING
· · · ·

A ball pitched to a green below your stance is more likely to stop than one pitched to a green above your stance.

56
· · · ·
CHIP AND RUN
· · · ·

The chip and run is played with a medium iron as opposed to the lofted club of the pitch. The ball is not played in such a lofted manner; it is only slightly lofted before landing and then running on to its intended target.

The leading edge should be square to the ball and ball-to-target line. Shorten the club slightly by moving your hands down the grip. You also want to take the loft off the club by holding your hands slightly forward at address. You want to open your stance and shift your bodyweight slightly on to your left leg.

57

· · · ·

WHERE TO AIM WHEN PITCHING AND CHIPPING

· · · ·

When chipping, a low running ball is the aim. De-loft the club by having the ball by the right heel and note that the take-away is one-piece. There should be little wrist break

When pitching it is advisable to use the flag as your aiming point. By doing this you are allowing for the ball, because of its trajectory, to drop into an area around the hole. When chipping, you want to use the hole as your aiming point.

58

REPAIRING PITCH MARKS AND DIVOTS

The divot is very much a part of some golf shots. Just because you take a divot with your shot doesn't mean you have played a bad stroke. However, if you do take a divot you must replace it and tread it back into its original place to give the grass a chance to grow again. If you see other divots which have not been replaced then don't leave them, put them back and play your part in maintaining the course.

It is obvious how much work goes into producing and maintaining the high quality of the putting surface. So, if your ball pitches onto the green, make sure you repair the pitch-mark with a pitch fork. And again, if you see somebody else's unrepaired pitch, then take the time to repair it.

Unlike when playing the pitch, the ball starts out with low flight

The follow-through is quite short because no more effort is being used than in putting

This is the so-called 'poached egg' lie. Think of sending both sand and ball out of the bunker

Out flies sand and ball

59
. . . .
PLAYING OUT OF A GREENSIDE BUNKER
. . . .

Before you enter the bunker, stand behind your ball and assess the shot you have to play. It is easier to get an idea of distance of your shot from outside the bunker than when you are stood in it.

A normal grip should be adopted when playing out of sand, but you should open your stance. Make sure your feet are comfortable in the sand and wriggle them into position before you address the ball, which should be positioned opposite your left heel. An open club face should be adopted.

Your shoulders should follow the line of your open stance and not be square to the ball-to-target line. Your backswing should be along the line of your shoulders and *not* along the line of the ball-to-target line. The backswing should be a wrist and arms action, and with a varying amount of body movement.

Concentrate your eyes on a position approximately 2in (5cm) behind the ball; it is this area the clubhead is going to strike.

There is a full follow-through. Don't just stop the clubhead in the sand. Instead, cut under the ball and go through with the shot

Because the club face is open, it travels under the sand and lifts the ball out of the bunker.

The amount of sand you take behind the ball depends on the distance the ball has to travel. The greater the distance, the less sand you take, and vice versa.

60
· · · ·
PLAYING FROM THE UPSLOPE OF THE BUNKER
· · · ·

Quite often, the big problem with this bunker shot is catching the lip of the trap with the ball. To overcome this problem you want to adopt a very open stance. However, it is equally important that you balance yourself well because one leg will be positioned higher than the other. Thereafter, the shot is very similar to playing the uphill lie off the fairway. Make sure you transfer plenty of weight onto your left leg.

A quick gain in height is needed to clear the lip of the bunker. Open your stance

From this plugged lie, the clubface is closed to help prevent it opening too far as it swings through the sand

The club is raised in a very upright path to avoid catching the back lip of the bunker

61
. . . .
PLAYING A BALL PLUGGED IN SAND
. . . .

This time you *don't* open your stance but play with a normal square stance, the ball positioned level with a point midway between your two feet.

The secret in getting the ball out of the sand now lies in playing a violent shot with a **closed** club face. The soft sand (it wouldn't have plugged if the sand was hard) will cause the clubface to open on impact.

You must try and create a follow through, but this depends upon the lie of the ball and how deeply it is plugged.

62
. . . .
PLAYING FROM THE BACK OF THE BUNKER
. . . .

Probably the worst type of bunker shot is the one with your ball at the very back of the bunker. There are two problems: firstly, you cannot get a good stance and secondly, the back of the bunker may hamper the clubhead in the back- and downswing.

You may have to stand with both feet outside the bunker or with one foot in, and the other out. Either way, you must create a very upright backswing to prevent the club hitting the back of the bunker. The upright backswing will create an open club face and it is important that you follow through after impact.

63
. . . .
PLAYING OUT OF FAIRWAY BUNKERS
. . . .

We have used the word 'ambition' several times before. But never is it as important as now, when you come to play a shot from a fairway bunker. How often does your ball seem to be sitting up nicely in the sand and with 150 yards to go to the green you optimistically take a 3-iron from your bag and hope to hit the

target, and what happens? The ball hits the lip of the bunker and drops back into the trap.

The actual stroke from a fairway bunker is not a difficult one, but you are well advised to take a club no stronger than a six- or seven-iron. You must always consider your next shot.

Make sure you have a firm hold, position your body square to the ball-to-target line (it doesn't need to be open this time) and focus your eyes on the ball, not the sand behind it, because this time you are playing the ball and not the sand.

64
• • • •
BUNKER ETIQUETTE
• • • •

When entering a bunker do so from the back of it and not the front. When you leave the bunker, make sure you rake over any footprints you may have left in the sand. If you don't then you are leaving footprints into which somebody else's ball can land. Don't forget you are not allowed to touch the sand with your club before playing your shot. If you do, you will be penalized two shots in stroke play and will lose the hole in matchplay.

The ball is against the centre of the clubface which is square with the line to the hole

65
• • • •
PUTTING BASICS
• • • •

The following are simple, but very important, basic principles of putting:
  (1) Make sure you have a sound hold of the club
  (2) Line your ball up square with the face of the putter and make sure it is in the centre of the club face
  (3) Keep the club face at right angles to the ground and square to your point of aim
  (4) Your eyes must be over the ball and your head must be still throughout the stroke
  (5) Don't let your wrists break
Follow those simple guidelines and you are more than halfway toward becoming a good player on the putting surface. And don't forget: all putts are straight, it is the borrow and speed which determine the direction.

66

. . . .

PUTTING: THE HOLD

. . . .

The hold you adopt for the putting stroke is very different to your normal hold. The most popular hold these days is the **reverse overlap** but with a selection of 'big' putters being seen all the time, holds have to be manufactured to fit the clubs. We will deal with the conventional putter and the reverse overlap.

All your fingers and thumbs, with one exception, grip the club handle to make sure you have a firm hold which enables you to move the putter accurately.

The four fingers and thumb of your right hand should grip the handle, with the thumb on the flattened part of the handle. The first three fingers of your left hand also grip the handle and the thumb of this hand is also placed on the flattened part of the handle. The only finger which does not make contact with the handle is the index finger of your right hand. It rests along the tops of the fingers of your right hand . . . it has to go somewhere!

A good secure hold like this will not only aid the accurate movement of the putter but will prevent you cocking your wrists. The putting stroke is made with the shoulders, arms, and putter moving as one unit; it is not a 'wristy' stroke.

No wrist break with this putting stroke. It is a shoulder and arms movement

The reverse overlap putting hold seen first from in front of the player and then a chest-on view

67

. . . .

BALL POSITION AT ADDRESS WHEN PUTTING

. . . .

To encourage a top-spin strike of the ball, it should ideally be opposite your left foot at address, but this depends on your individual putting style. If you watch the professionals, you will see there is a wide variety in personal putting styles, but you are best to stick to the conventional putting method until you gain more confidence and are ready to experiment.

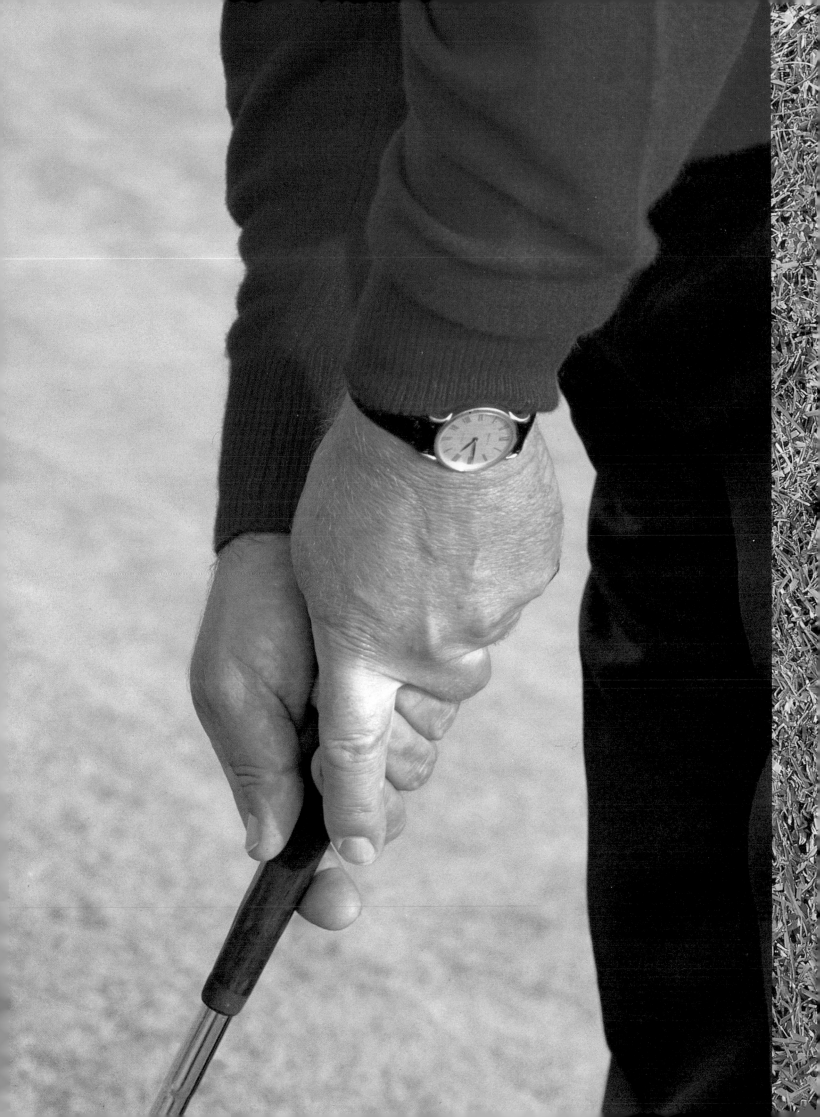

68
· · · ·
PUTTING POSTURE
· · · ·

When putting you need to adopt a good posture. The width of your stance varies according to individual style, but ideally, the outside of your shoes should be level with your shoulders.

At address your head and eyes should be directly over the ball. Consequently, you need to bend at the waist with your bodyweight evenly distributed between both feet. Balance, posture and weight distribution are very important factors in playing the putting stroke because you must make sure your head and body are kept still during the stroke. And remember, the stroke is made with the arms, shoulders, and club only.

In this stance, the outsides of the shoes are level with the shoulders

69

· · · ·

PUTTING: PRACTICE AND AMBITION

· · · ·

The putting stroke is the one that can make or break a good round. Strokes can be gained or lost on the putting surface, so spend a little time practising your putting stroke before a round. Don't expect to reach the first green and know its pace. Even the best players are not that good judges.

Practice greens are there for the purpose of practising, so take advantage of them. They will give a good indication as to how the real greens are playing; fast or slow.

That word 'ambition' is back again. And it applies to the putting stroke as much as it does to playing out of long rough, bunkers and so on.

When faced with a monster 40-foot putt you want to assess realistically your chance of holing the putt. Invariably, it will be slim. In that case your ambition must be to get the ball as near the hole as possible so as to make your next putt easier. Set yourself a target of two putts on each green. If the odd long putt goes down first time then it's a bonus. But don't forget there will be times when you miss those easy putts from nine inches . . .

Club and forearms are in more-or-less a straight line

70

· · · ·

CONFIDENCE ON THE PUTTING GREEN

· · · ·

Putting skills require so many fundamentally correct skills; touch, reading the green, assessing the speed of the putt and concentration. But there is another very important element – confidence. This word applies to every golf shot, but in particular the one on the putting surface where the difference between success and failure is so very obvious.

You must have confidence in your ability to putt. If you haven't then I'm afraid you are going to lose valuable strokes on each round.

To build your confidence you want to practice this part of your game probably more than any other. Certainly spend some time on the practice greens before every round.

71
. . . .
READING GREENS
. . . .

The inability to 'read' a green will cost you many important strokes during a round of golf. All greens are magnificently manicured by green keepers, and every green is individual. They may all appear to be beautifully level with a pool-table appearance. But look closely at any green and you will see a series of borrows. You must be able to identify these borrows and assess which way they turn and how the roll of your ball across the putting surface will be affected by such a borrow. You must read the green.

If there is a severe borrow which will take your ball to the right of the hole, then clearly you must aim to the left of the hole. However, it is not solely the severity of the borrow which determines how much you aim to the left but *speed also determines borrow.* The faster you hit the ball, the less effect the borrow will have. So, it is important that you assess the speed of your putt as well.

To determine a borrow, stand behind your ball and look toward the hole, then make up your mind where your point of aim is and take up your address. Don't change your mind . . . it's often fatal.

A green surrounded by glittering sand at Sea Pines in South Carolina

72
. . . .
PUTTING GREEN ETIQUETTE AND RULES
. . . .

The putting surface takes many years to get into perfect condition, and many hours of hard work to maintain it. So, firstly, please remember that and treat it with utmost respect. If you have made any pitch marks on the green then repair them. If somebody else has made a pitch mark and not repaired it then don't leave it, repair it for them.

If you are putting and your ball is already on the putting surface the flag must be out of the hole or attended to by another person while you putt, but they must remove it once your ball has been struck. However, if you are putting and your ball is off the putting surface then you can choose between having the flag in, out, or attended. When taking the flag out, don't throw it to the putting surface, place it carefully on the ground.

Don't stand in somebody's line of sight when they are putting and keep perfectly still and quiet while another player is putting.

This applies at all times, not just on the putting surface, for reasons of safety as well as fair play.

Finally, as you approach the green, bear in mind where you have to leave it as you walk to the next hole and leave your bag at an exit point near to the next tee. There is nothing more infuriating than waiting to play your next shot to a green while a disorganized group walk to different points around the green to collect their bags. Incidentally, you shouldn't put your bags or trolleys on to the putting surface.

73

PREPARING FOR BAD WEATHER

Unlike cricket, rain doesn't stop play in golf. So you must be ready for the worst the elements can throw at you: or alternatively, you can go home! But that is a defeatist attitude.

You should make sure you always carry a good set of water-proofs in your golf bag, and have them ready to put on at the first sign of rain. But don't make the mistake, as so many people do, of putting the waterproofs on over your normal clothing without first taking essential items like tees, pencil, pitch forks, etc, out of your pockets. There is nothing more embarassing than having to take your waterproofs off again in order to get at these items.

Obviously, you will also need an umbrella to protect you in the rain; but the one thing many novice golfers ignore in adverse weather conditions is the **chill factor.** Make sure you keep yourself warm. There is nothing worse for your swing than a cold body and cold muscles. A spare sweater and a hat are useful additions to your golfing attire.

It is also useful to carry a towel in your bag and whatever you do, make sure you keep your hands dry and warm. Wet and cold hands will have a disastrous effect on your hold.

74

PLAYING IN WIND

You can't see the wind. It may not be there one minute, and the next it appears. It may be a headwind on one hole, or a side wind on another. Wind was invented to make the golfer's life a misery.

Unfortunately, you can never take on and beat the wind. But what you must do is make allowances for it. If you played a shot to a hole with, say, a 5-iron last week, but this week have a strong headwind on the same hole, then don't take the 5-iron again and expect to play the same shot: you must make allowances and take, perhaps, a 3-iron.

The wind won't only affect the flight of your ball, but will also throw your swing off balance if it is strong enough. To help your swing in windy conditions, move your hands an inch or two (2½–5cm) down the grip and compensate for this in your stance.

The famous short 7th hole at Pebble Beach

75

· · · ·

PLAYING WITH THE WIND

· · · ·

These conditions can be very advantageous to you becuse, with the wind behind you, your ball is going to travel further. For that reason, you must take a more lofted club than you would normally have taken. Only the strength of the wind and distance to the green will dictate your choice of club, but beware not to take a club with insufficient loft because if you do, the wind may carry your ball through the green and possibly into all sorts of trouble.

76

. . . .

PLAYING INTO A HEADWIND

. . . .

The opposite rules now apply. You want to take a less lofted club so that you keep your ball lower. If you take a club that is too lofted, then your ball will sail high into the air but won't travel far enough forward.

However, playing into a headwind when pitching to a green can be an advantage because you can, with the use of a lofted club, create a higher trajectory and therefore get the ball to hang in the air longer than usual before dropping onto its intended target.

Waterproofs should not be too tight fitting, especially under the arms and across the shoulders

77

. . . .

PLAYING IN A CROSSWIND

. . . .

The left-to-right wind is regarded as the worst type of wind condition the right-handed player can play in. Obviously, the right-to-left wind is the worst for the left-handed player.

Because the wind is blowing at your back it will invariably throw you off balance. Consequently, you want to make sure you adopt a firm stance. Because of the strength of the wind your ball is going to be blown from the left to the right while in flight so you must aim sufficiently to the left to compensate. However, you *must* make sure you hit the ball straight and let the wind do the rest. If you slice or hook, or pull or push in such conditions, then you can expect a lot of problems. When playing with a right-to-left wind then you should this time aim your ball to the right of its target, and again make sure you hit it straight.

78

· · · ·

PLAYING IN RAIN

· · · ·

We have already told you about the merits of wearing good waterproofs and preparing yourself before you put them on. It is not often easy, but you should try and keep yourself as dry as possible. You should also ensure that you keep your clubs, particularly the grips, dry. You don't need to be told what can happen if you attempt to play a shot with a wet grip.

Also, make sure you keep your hands dry and if you are wearing a glove keep it protected while you are not playing a shot. You can buy all-weather gloves which don't absorb the rain as much as conventional leather ones. They are a wise investment.

Two other points to remember about playing in the rain: (1) The ground will be slippery, so make sure your shoes are well studded, and (2) Rainwater gathers on a golf ball. You are not allowed to dry your ball until it is on the putting surface. When playing from the fairway, the water will not go until the ball gets airborne. Therefore you want to get the ball airborne quicker than normal. The use of a slightly more lofted club will achieve this and probably not lose you any distance with your shot, because one will compensate for the other.

Ready to beat wind and rain

79

· · · ·

PLAYING IN THUNDER AND LIGHTNING

· · · ·

The best tip in such conditions is *get off the course*. However, if that is not immediately practicable, then these are two very important DONT'S.

   (1) Don't put your umbrella up, unless you have a modern one with built-in safety measures.
   (2) Don't shelter under a tree.

80

. . . .

CURING THE SLICE

. . . .

If you look at the following list of possible causes of the slice you will appreciate why the slice creeps into so many players' game.

The possible causes are:

(1) The club face is open when making contact with the ball. This is because the leading edge is open and as we emphasized earlier the leading edge must *always* be square to the ball and ball-to-target line at impact. This is the most common cause of the slice.

(2) The club face is opened too quickly in the takeaway

(3) An out-to-in swing is created because the club is taken away on the **outside** (see tip 30).

(4) There is a weak hold on the club which is often caused by one or both hands being too far around the grip.

(5) The shoulders are open at address, often caused by positioning the ball too far forward.

81

. . . .

THE SLICE: INCORRECT BALL POSITION AND ADDRESS

. . . .

Having the ball too far forward and level with the left toe is a likely cause of the slice. It should be positioned level with the left heel if using a wooden club. Because the ball is too far forward, so are the hands at address.

However, if you set the ball in the correct position, but then adopt an open stance, you can expect a sliced shot.

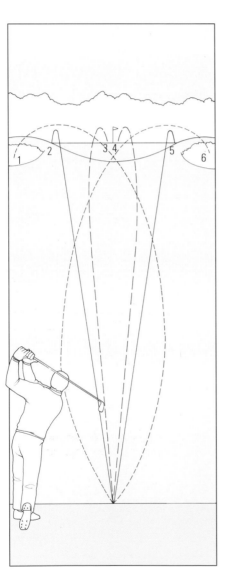

1. Hook   4. Draw
2. Pull   5. Push
3. Fade   6. Slice

82

• • • •

THE SLICE: AN INCORRECT HOLD

• • • •

A weak hold is a very common cause of the slice. One or both hand are too far round the handle of the club. This will contribute towards the opening of the club face at impact which will cause the slice.

LEFT This very open stance would almost certainly cause a slice

ABOVE The stance is now more square but this weak hold would cause slicing

83

· · · ·

CURING THE HOOK

· · · ·

Like the slice, there are many possible causes of the hook. If it has crept into your game then look down this list; there is probably a cause which you can identify, and hopefully rectify.

(1) The biggest cause of the hook is having the leading edge turned inward at impact ie the club face is closed. Moving the hands too far forward at the address can cause the club face to become closed.

(2) You create an **in-to-out** swing path (see tip 30).

(3) At the top of the backswing the club has gone over the target line and is aiming to the right of the target.

(4) The right elbow is held too close to the body in the back-swing and downswing.

(5) A **strong** hold is adopted. In other words one or both hands are too far to the right on the grip.

(6) The shoulders are closed at address, often caused by having the ball positioned too far back.

Both hands here are in a very weak position

84

· · · ·

THE HOOK: AN INCORRECT HOLD

· · · ·

Unlike the slice, a strong hold is a probable cause of the hook. This time, one or both hands are too far to the right and not far enough around the handle.

A strong hold again. The ball is also too far back in the stance, causing the shoulders to be in a closed position

The hold on the club is now far too strong, sure cause of hooking

85

· · · ·

THE HOOK: INCORRECT BALL POSITION AND ADDRESS

· · · ·

Positioning the ball too far back at address is one of the most common causes of the hook; because it is so far back there is a good chance that the club face will be closed at impact. While you are trying to get your head behind the ball, which is now too far back, you are distorting your body and it is no shape to manufacture an ideal golf swing. Closing the stance too much at address is also a possible cause of the hook.

86

· · · ·

TOPPING: THE CAUSES

· · · ·

A strong hold on the club causes the shoulders to look, and feel, cramped

Topping is that embarrassing shot which most novices make at some time. Proper contact is not made with the ball and it is hit toward the top. Consequently it doesn't get airborne. Newcomers to golf are under the impression the ball should be lifted into the air. It is not. The loft on the club is so designed to do that for you.

However, topping does happen. If it is happening to you then take a look at these possible causes:

(1) The ball is too far forward at address.

(2) If playing the ball off the tee it is not teed up high enough.

(3) You are standing too far away from the ball.

(4) Your head comes up at impact, normally caused by a poor weight distribution with your weight being transferred to your left leg on the backswing and to your right leg on the downswing.

(5) The collapsing of the left arm at the top of the backswing.

(6) Your hold on the club is too tight, causing a tension which results in the body being lifted at the moment of contact.

(7) Of course, playing with the wrong club can cause the ball to be topped. If your ball is plugged into a wet fairway then you wouldn't contemplate taking a driver out of your bag. You would use a medium or short iron.

87

. . . .

FLUFFING: THE CAUSES

. . . .

Fluffing is as embarassing to the novice golfer as topping. Fluffing occurs when the clubhead strikes the ground before making contact with the ball. It happens because the downswing is too steep and consequently so is the attack by the clubhead on the golf ball.

The most common cause of fluffing is having the ball positioned too far back at address. As a result your shoulders tilt and cause your arms to go too high in the air in the backswing and also transfer too much weight onto your left leg. If you let the club travel further than your body turns, then you will find yourself stabbing at the ball at impact and this will again cause fluffing.

88

. . . .

RECOGNIZING FAULTS

. . . .

It is easy to say; "I'm slicing because the club face is open at address". Indeed that is probably why you are slicing. But that is not the whole story. You have to find out *why* the club face is open at address and that may be because your right shoulder is turning too high, which causes the out-to-in swing path, which in turn causes your hands to be ahead of the ball at impact, opening the club face.

So it's no use identifying the obvious cause of the slice, or whatever error has crept into your game. You must go back and look at *all* the possible causes. Please remember *most faults can be found in the address position.* So use that as the starting point when looking for faults.

89

. . . .

CONSIDERATION FOR OTHER GOLFERS

. . . .

Golf can be a dangerous game if played negligently and without due consideration for other golfers out on the course. Be aware of what is going on around you at all times. Don't play a shot until the match in front of you is well out of range. However, if your ball appears to be travelling in the direction of another player then you must shout the acknowledged warning of 'fore!'.

Nothing but the best of manners is acceptable on the golf course and the game should be played in the best spirit. Don't talk, move, or make a noise while another player is about to play a shot, and don't tee your ball up on the teeing ground until the other players have taken their shot in the correct rotational order.

Don't waste time either. Get on with your game as quickly as the match in front allows, and when you have putted out, don't stand around discussing the hole with your playing partners.

90

· · · ·

ALWAYS PLAY THE PROVISIONAL BALL

· · · ·

If there is a chance that your ball will be lost, or may be out-of-bounds, then you should always play a provisional ball. You will not be penalized if your original ball is found and is playable. But if it is not, then you have to go back to where the shot was played, in order to try again, so you may as well play the provisional ball. That is why the rules allow the playing of such a ball. However, if your first ball isn't found, then you must play the provisional ball from where it lies, under penalty.

91

· · · ·

DROPPING YOUR BALL

· · · ·

If you are forced to drop your ball because it is unplayable you should first establish whether you are dropping under penalty or not. But either way, you should know how to drop your ball according to the rules.

Until recently it used to be dropped over the shoulder. But these days the ball is dropped from arm's length and shoulder height in front of you. The ball must be dropped as near to its original position as possible but not *nearer* the hole. After dropping, it must come to rest within two club-lengths of the point where it first hit the ground. If this distance is in doubt and you have to measure it, then use the longest club in your bag.

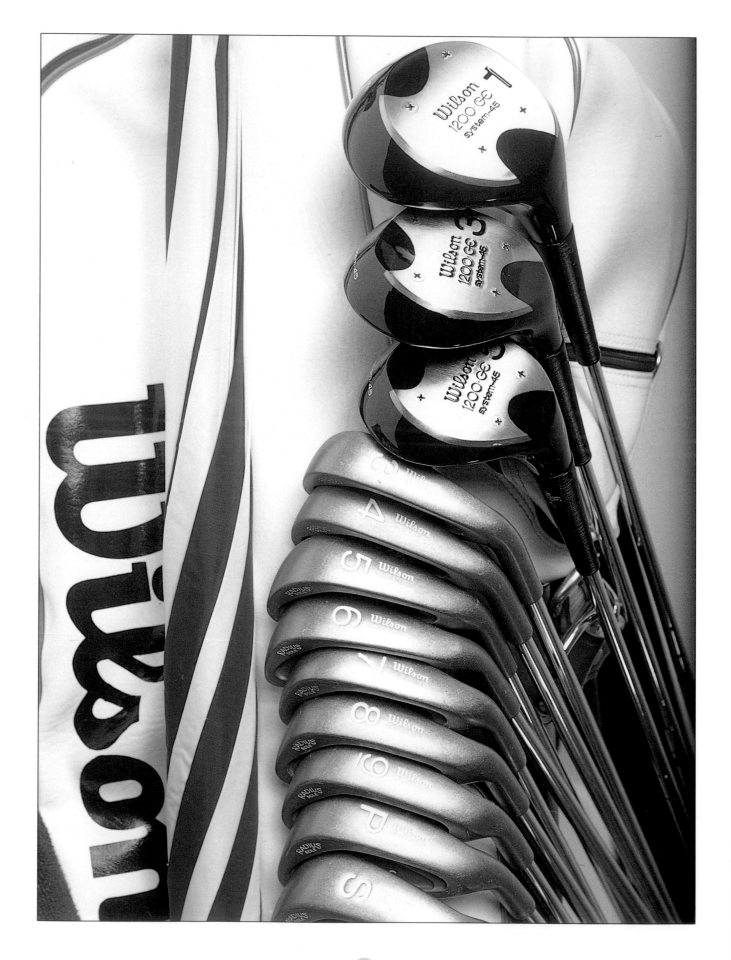

92

. . . .

FIRST TO PLAY

. . . .

The 'honour' to play first in golf is something that has to be won, and the order of play and the honour to go first must be strictly adhered to during a game. It is important that you understand the official ruling.

The honour at the first tee has to be decided by lots or the toss of a coin. Thereafter the side winning the hole has the honour of playing first at the next hole and so on.

If you are playing stroke-play then the person with the lowest score at the next hole goes first, and the second lowest score goes next, and so on. If any scores are level then the same order of play is maintained.

In match-play the side who wins the hole goes first at the next. In the event of a halved hole, then the honour remains with the side who had it on the halved hole.

In all instances, when playing a ball other than from the teeing area, the person whose ball is furthest away from the hole plays first.

93

. . . .

BUYING GOLF CLUBS

. . . .

Golf clubs come in varying sizes. It is important that you select the right clubs for *you*. Don't assume all golf clubs are the same, they are not. No doubt you will have looked through a golf magazine and been confronted with dozens of advertisements for clubs. So which ones should you pick when buying a new set?

The answer is simple; within your own budget, buy clubs that fit your physical needs. Your height affects the lie of the club and consequently has an effect on the leading edge – the most important part of the golf club. If you buy the wrong clubs you could find the heel or toe of the clubhead making contact with the ground when you play a shot.

The only way to make sure you are selecting the right clubs is by seeking advice, and that is best given by a PGA professional. You would seek advice from a tailor when buying a suit; buying golf clubs is no different. Your local professional will probably have some trial clubs for you to try out on the practice ground.

It is possible to buy just one secondhand club with which to begin learning the game – a 5-iron is fine – along with a putter. By hiring or borrowing clubs at the outset, you will not find yourself stuck with expensive equipment not suited to your game at a later date

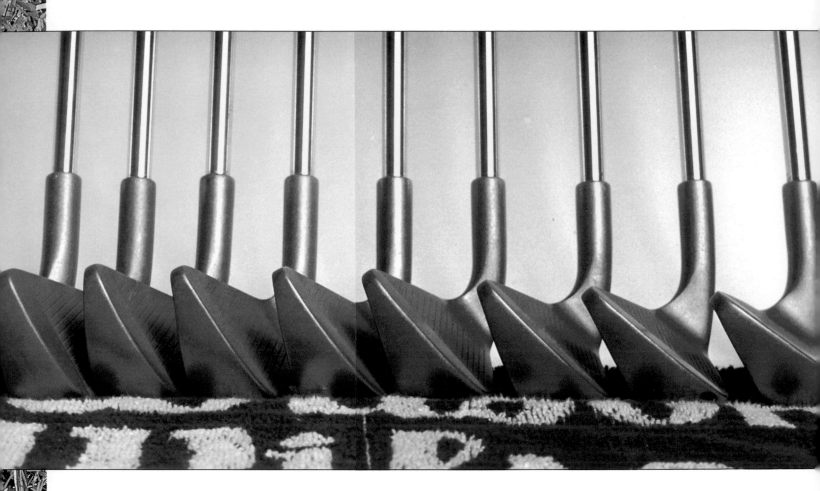

94

. . . .

LOOKING AFTER YOUR CLUBS

. . . .

They say a poor workman blames his tools. But if you allow your clubs to deteriorate then those 'tools' won't do the job properly for you, through your own fault.

You should always make sure the grooves on the club face are regularly cleaned out. They amass quite a lot of dirt during a round of golf and the grooves are not there just to gather dirt, they serve a purpose as an aid to the flight of the golf ball. Dirty grooves won't do their job properly. Furthermore, they will cause damage to the ball.

Make sure the grips of your clubs are kept clean. If they aren't then your hold on the club will be affected. When storing your clubs, be careful where you put them. Don't leave them in a position where other heavy articles can be piled on top of them. And if you leave your clubs in the boot of your car make sure they have plenty of room and are not crammed in, causing the shafts to bend.

95

GOLF BALLS

You will have noticed that all golf balls, apart from having the name of the manufacturer on them, also have a number for identification purposes, to enable players to spot their own ball quickly.

Many players believe that the higher the number, the better the ball. This is a complete fallacy. But if your mind tells you that you play better with a No.4 then by all means use a No.4 . . . after all, a lot of golf is played in the mind.

You'd be surprised how many matches start without players consulting each other about the type or number of ball being used. When two players go looking for lost balls they'll both discover they're using the same make and number of ball! So, consult with your partner or opponents before each round. However, two players can play with the same make of ball, and indeed same number, provided one, or both, marks the ball with a pen. Most professionals will mark a ball with their own characteristic marking by filling in a dimple or dimples.

96

CLOTHING

Golfing etiquette and rules must be obeyed at all times. And in particular rules about dress must be strictly adhered to, both on the course and in the clubhouse.

Most courses will not allow the wearing of jeans and certainly not track shoes. Shorts are also outlawed by many clubs in warm weather, but others are relaxing their rules on this subject and if, like Brian Barnes, you are more relaxed wearing shorts in warm weather, then check the local rules before you play.

In the clubhouse you may be requested to wear a tie and/or a jacket, so, if you want to enjoy the hospitality of the 19th after your round of golf, make sure you have both with you.

ABOVE The Balata ball has a rubber centre which is filled with water before rubber bands are wound around it

BELOW The Surlyn covered ball with a solid rubber centre

The beauty of the golf courses themselves is
part of the attraction of the game

97

JOINING A GOLF CLUB

Joining a golf club is often a lengthy process. You normally have to be recommended and seconded for membership but in many cases waiting for a vacancy takes a long time.

If you want to join a club you are well advised to put your name forward as early as possibly and then be patient. You can, of course, in the meantime, play your golf on municipal courses or can play as a visitor at a private club.

98

BELIEVE IN YOURSELF

Quite often you will be faced with a shot and secretly tell yourself you can't play the shot. This lack of self-confidence will probably then tell in the shot and you *won't* play it. But if you have done everything right, and selected the right club, then there is no reason why you shouldn't be able to play the shot confronting you – unless you are being over-ambitious of course!

So, believe in yourself. And the more often you successfully make those seemingly 'impossible' shots, the better you will become. *Then* you can become more ambitious.

99

KEEP A DIARY

Most golfers with handicaps in excess of 20 probably play golf once a week, at the most. They will pack their clubs in their car, spend three and a half or four hours enjoying the round and forget all about it until the next time.

But if you want to improve your game and see where you are (or are not) making progress, you are well advised to keep a diary of all your rounds. Make a note of not only your scores, but how many greens you hit in regulation (don't forget you should hit a par three in one shot, a par four in two, and a par five in three shots), and how many fairways you hit off the tee. Also, make a note of how many putts you take on each hole.

It is a good idea to split every round you play into three parts, each lasting six holes. Aim for a score of 30 on each six and if, say, you shoot a 32 on the first six holes, then aim for a 28 on the next six in order to pull back those lost strokes. However, if you score 28 on the first six don't think you can ease off and aim for 32 on the next . . . try and shoot another 28. After a few weeks, analyze that lot and you will clearly see what kind of progress (or otherwise) you are making.

100
. . . .
NEVER BE AFRAID TO APPROACH A GOLF PROFESSIONAL
. . . .

Golfers who know go to their pro

PGA Professionals are not here just to run their pro shops or give golf lessons. They are here to offer advice to the golfing public. Don't be afraid to approach your PGA professional, he will be only too pleased to help in any way he can. You don't even have to be a member of a club to seek advice and help from a professional.

Professionals sell a wide range of golfing equipment, and will give you the correct advice on purchases. Many newcomers will often buy a set, or half set, of clubs by mail order and expect the clubs to be suitable for them. Your own individual make-up dictates the clubs you should buy, and only professional advice can guide you on this matter.

Regarding advice on golf techniques, all golfers should at some stage of their development seek advice from a professional who can instantly see what you are doing wrong and can help rectify your faults. Even if you have been playing golf for a few years, it never does any harm to return to your professional for a refresher course.

So, don't be afraid to approach your professional. He's a nice friendly guy and he has the interest of the game of golf and its players at heart. You cannot go to any better person for advice about the sport.

INDEX